RITA O'HARE

RITA

Greenisland Press

This edition published in 2024
Greenisland Press, Belfast
e-mail: info@greenislandpress.ie

An imprint of Elsinor Verlag (Elsinor Press), Coesfeld, Germany
e-mail: info@elsinor.de
website: www.elsinor.de

Cover design: Seán Mistéil; photo, Brendan Brownlee
Printed in Germany

ISBN: 978-3-949573-07-1

To my Brendan; to Terry, Frances, Rory and Ciaran;
our grandchildren—Kevin, Aidan, Aoife, Naoise, Dualta, Luke,
Caolainn, Sinéad, Meadhbh, Emma, Conall;
and to our great grandchildren—Kate, Keelin, Mason, Fionntan,
Luiseach, Cathal, Rioghnach, Oisín, and Ríadh

CONTENTS

Rita and Brendan at home

FOREWORD

Rita O'Hare died on 3 March, 2023, after a long battle with cancer. For some time I had been haranguing her to write a memoir. Rita was not easy to harangue. She resisted my entreaties. But I persisted, because she had an important and a remarkable story to tell, and I believe in people telling their own stories. This is important everywhere. But especially in Ireland in these post-conflict times. By setting our different narratives side by side we have the possibility of a more complete and inclusive insight into the past and how and why conflict occurred. And how it might be avoided.

Eventually Rita relented. She agreed to start writing. I think the persuasive argument was: 'Do it for your family.' So she did. Michael Nolan helped enormously by taping and transcribing Rita's words when she was too tired or sick to type or scribble her recollections. Danny Morrison assisted also. As did Síle Darragh with the transcriptions.

But unfortunately Rita left it too late. She ran out of time. So it fell to Danny Morrison to edit her manuscript. Danny has done Rita and us all a great service.

When I first read the final draft I thought of it as an incomplete memoir. There are gaps. It ends too soon. There are people who do not feature who certainly would feature if Rita had had the time to revise her writing, and others who would have featured more fully. But none of this is deliberate. For all her fierceness Rita valued the connections she had with many, many people, particularly her friends and comrades. So I am sure she would love to have written a more comprehensive account. But it was not to be and Danny's editing stays true to her voice and text.

Rita's qualities included guidance, direction, an unwavering presence, and a lifelong commitment to the struggle for Irish independence and freedom.

If this is an incomplete political memoir it is a very complete personal one—especially in relation to Brendan and the family, the

9

children, the grandchildren, great grandchildren, and, of course, to her parents, Maureen and Billy. This is Rita reaching out to them, setting out her regrets and insights, thanking them and hugging each and every one of them. I am sure they will be moved by the obvious sincerity and genuine way that she does this.

Others will be less pleased.

Rita is scathing about those who presided over Ireland's inequalities, unfair systems, including the partition of our island and our people. She brings a particular and unique focus and perspective to this: as an Irish person, as a woman, as a survivor of a British Army ambush, as a mother of three small children who went to prison and later into exile in Dublin away from her home in Belfast, and then back to prison yet again. She was there throughout all the decades of building Sinn Féin and throughout the long, difficult search for peace, and she especially made her mark as our representative in North America.

There may be gaps in this narrative, as I have explained, but Rita writes well and the reader will get the sense of all that was entailed in these battles and a sense also of a great woman. Rita survived it all and died peacefully at home with her beloved Brendan and their clann, shortly after her eightieth birthday.

Defiant and hopeful to the end.

Gerry Adams, Belfast
July 2024

PROLOGUE

News started to circulate that the Brits were moving up the road into Andersonstown, taking down the barricades. I got word about it and went over to the estate to join the others. I remember it was a very cold night. The Brits had managed to get in from the top of the area, at Ramoan Gardens, after a lot of fighting and were making their way towards Kenard Avenue. There was huge resistance to them, and the battle went on for a long time.

I waited until there was a lull and thought it was safe to move. I was moving between houses when I saw a Brit Army Pig, an armoured car, turn into the street. Shots were fired and I ran down the side of a house and the next thing I felt was a big thump in my back and on my head. I actually thought that they had crept up behind me. I didn't realise that I'd been shot. I fell and lost consciousness. It seemed like only seconds. When I opened my eyes, soldiers stood all around me. They were very young and absolutely terrified.

One of them hit me in the face, twice, with a rifle butt; smashed my teeth on either side of my face. I thought my nose was broken. Another was shouting orders for them to get off the street, to get back to the Pig. A few of them grabbed me by the arms and legs and ran with me, half-dragging me over to the armoured car. It was then I felt the pain knifing through me. They were hysterical with fear that they were going to come under further attack, and I learned later that one of them had been wounded shortly beforehand. Some of them started kicking me, punching me and hitting me again and I'll never forget one of them kneeling over me to protect me and told them to stop it. He put his hand under my head to stop it banging off the bottom of the Pig. And when he took his hand away it was covered in blood. It was then that I realised how badly injured I was.

They took me first to Musgrave Park Military Hospital. When the doors of the Pig were opened there was a man, possibly a doctor, waiting. He looked in. When he opened my coat a jet of blood hit the

11

roof of the Pig. If it hadn't been for a big heavy duffel coat I was wearing I would have bled to death. He closed the coat back over me and said, 'Take her away.'

Who he was, I don't know, but it was obvious he thought I was going to die in their custody and it would be on their heads. Perhaps they didn't want that—another woman killed by British soldiers, forty-eight hours after they'd killed Dorothy and Maura.

The armoured car drove down the Falls Road and I realised they were taking me to the Royal Victoria Hospital. During the journey the same young soldier continued to try to stop the others from kicking me, saying there was no need for it.

I remember going into shock. I started shaking violently. Some of them started shouting: 'She's dying! Look, she's dying!'

Whether I said it out loud or not, I was saying to myself, 'I am not dying. I am not going to die.'

CHAPTER ONE

BILLY

I knew, even though none of this was discussed around the family table, that there was something wrong from an early age, that things were not normal. You would have had to have been very unaware of your surroundings if you didn't recognise by the time you were thirteen or fourteen that there was a despondency attached to the place, a gloom, a weight. I couldn't have articulated it then but it was a sense of victors and vanquished, in the way that everything was arranged, in the way that even the news, sport, culture, was presented on television. For many adults it was safer to live with their head in the sand because the alternative meant having to do something about it, and the prospects of bringing about change were not only slim but came at a cost.

Though I did not come from a nationalist or republican or wholly Catholic family I was very politically aware.

My father Billy McCulloch was the biggest influence in my life—from politics to literature, music ... everything.

We lived in a semi-detached house in Norfolk Drive, off the Glen Road in Andersonstown. Most of our neighbours were middle-class Catholics—teachers, accountants, bank officials, engineers, an auctioneer, draughtsman, clerk, chemist. They didn't want trouble. Just wanted to get on with their own lives within the prevailing anti-Irish, anti-Catholic culture. There was a barman lived next door, but he would have been the most ordinary working-class person that I can remember. The men went to work and the wives stayed at home looking after the children, as most women did in those days. I'm not saying people weren't nice, but nobody really interacted with each other. The street had no discernible 'politics' as such. There would have been one or two families that spoke Irish or were into the GAA but they were a minority. I was not aware of anybody in that street espousing left-wing or republican politics. If there were republicans, they certainly kept it quiet, probably being security conscious for good reason.

Opposite Norfolk was Andersonstown RUC barracks and a few policemen also lived in our and surrounding streets.

Catholics had their church but because our family weren't part of it I wasn't aware to what extent the rest of the neighbours interacted with or depended on it. People talk about belonging to the community but there wasn't a community to belong to, unlike further down the Falls and the Pound Loney which had experienced conflict and been attacked by Orangemen as far back as the 1850s. It was the working-class areas that experienced or showed a sense of communal solidarity and were keenest about their Irishness.

Billy was an internationalist. He believed passionately in equality and in the distribution of wealth, rejected the very notion of monarchy and privilege and hated sectarianism and bigotry.

He was born in Rosebery Road in East Belfast and joined the Communist Party when he was seventeen, which was really young. This was at a time when the rallying cry was 'Workers Unite'. He knew all the old Belfast commies. But the party was small, and it was split because the national question affected everything. He claimed he had a memory of hearing James Connolly speak in Belfast. He would have been only three at the time, so I don't know if he was mistaken. He was also an avowed atheist—and that was also unusual in those days. I remember him turning to me when I was about six, we were walking in the Falls Park and were having a conversation, and Billy just turned to me and said, 'Just remember, God's a cod!' And I've never forgotten. He taught us the words of the *Red Flag*, but my younger brother Bill was the only one who inherited our mother's musical talent, so he was the only one who could sing it. We all went to piano lessons, and we could hit the right notes at close to the right times, but it was Bill who could play. Really play. Not just piano but other instruments too.

Billy's parents had been Protestant immigrants. His father, John William McCulloch, originally from Scotland, was a merchant seaman and when he met Mary Frances, a domestic servant from Conah's Quay in Wales, he didn't want to go back to sea and leave her. He worked as an iron-moulder in Birkenhead during the engineering boom in the 1880s. He heard that there were jobs going in Belfast in the shipyard (for 'good Protestant men') and that's how they ended up in Belfast even though they didn't have any connection to Ireland. They lived in unionist East

Belfast but he abhorred the Orange Order and wouldn't have anything to do with sectarianism. He was left-wing, an internationalist and a staunch trade unionist. Billy was the youngest of three sons and four daughters. Billy's sister Mimi was dating an Orangeman and he once asked Billy, who was just a kid, to help carry one of the banners on the Twelfth of July parade down the Ormeau Road, considered a great honour at the time. Billy never did it again; his father was so displeased.

My mother Maureen (McGinn) was Catholic, but her mother's background was even more Protestant than my father's, if you know what I mean. Though raised a Catholic in Ballymacarrett in East Belfast, Maureen wasn't a 'holy picture on the wall' Catholic, and Catholicism would never have been discussed in the house. My mother became religious only as she got older. Because of her background, the South was a foreign country to her. Her mother came from a sect in County Down called the Christian Brethren and they were very strict, very rigid Protestants. No-cooking-on-a-Sunday-type people. Maud, my Protestant grandmother, whose maiden name was Carnaghan, somehow managed to meet my grandfather, a Catholic from Killough. Nobody has ever figured out how they met. To say that her family were not pleased is putting it mildly. In the mid-1930s my maternal grandparents rented a holiday home in Coney Island across the inlet from Killough with a beautiful view of the Mournes, which they bought in the early Sixties.

My mother loved Coney Island. She loved the sea and was a strong swimmer. She swam in the sea whenever she could, into her eighties. The house has stayed in the family. My cousin Pat Freedman from Washington and her husband Moses bought it in 1992 and planned to retire there. I said to Pat, 'You'll never last a winter.'

But they have and they love it. They've now been there almost twenty years.

Billy and Maureen were married in 1939 and moved into Norfolk Drive in Andersonstown. They rented the house and actually didn't get buying it until the 1980s. During the Belfast blitz in WWII my mother and Alan, the first born, went to stay with my grandmother in South Belfast which was considered safer and that's where I was born in January 1943, in Marina Park, which is actually in County Down. My brother Alan was fourteen months my elder, and my brother Bill was two years younger.

Rita at a year old

Christmas 1961

Billy, Rita, Alan, Maureen and Bill, Norfolk Drive, c. late 1940s

Tullaree, Mournes

Maternal grandparents Maud and James McGinn, 1956

We had a terrific childhood. The Falls Park was at the top of our street. It was open twenty-four hours a day. Its iron railings had yet to be replaced having been removed and smelted down as part of the war effort. The park had an open-air swimming pool—the Cooler. I wasn't much of a swimmer but in those days, you just jumped in. There was no such concept as Health and Safety! It was originally fed from the Ballymurphy stream which still runs through the City Cemetery but the pool was closed in the seventies after a number of incidents, including a child drowning.

When it was time for our education Billy's view was that the best school is the nearest school and nearly always the nearest was a Catholic school. I remember in class hearing the teacher talk about the Pope and having no idea who or what they were talking about but being smart enough not to say anything. If everybody else knew who he was it must have been important and I wasn't going to make an eejit of myself.

There were two types of schools in the North: 'Controlled' which were associated with the state and seen as being Protestant, and 'Maintained' which were associated with the Catholic Church. In those days very few Catholics sent their kids to Protestant schools, even if they had thrown in their lot with 'Northern Ireland' out of hopes of personal aggrandizement, and might even vote unionist.

Catholic schooling inevitably contributed to one's sense of being Irish. But the Catholic schools were quite careful of what they taught about the North, terrified of accusations of being sectarian. The boys' schools were different because the Christian Brothers were much more open about republicanism.

In 1954 I passed the 11-plus and transferred to St Dominic's Grammar School on the Falls Road, most of whose pupils came from middle-class backgrounds, although I finished my A Levels at Rathmore Grammar.

I remember Billy giving me *The Grapes of Wrath* for my twelfth birthday. It was a novel I could relate to as I noticed the poverty and the desperation in Belfast: the need for the rights of workers, for free education, for a way to change their situation. Another present, when I was a bit older, was *The Wretched of the Earth* about colonisation.

When we weren't roaming the Falls Park, we were down in the Mourne Mountains in Tullaree. It was in the Mournes that my parents actually first met, in the Slievenamon Youth Hostel. They both had a romantic connection to the area. Billy loved the mountains and Maureen loved the sea. We rented a house from a local farmer. There was no electricity or running water, but we went there every holiday, except Christmas. My mother drew a line at that though she loved the place too.

Several times each day we had to fetch water from a well down from the house. Billy, in one of his famous fixing-up moments, invented something that could pump the water up the hill but we still had to use the buckets. My mother cooked on an open fire or on a camping stove and we had a Tilly lamp for light. She used to make bread on a big griddle. We used to help her carry a tin bath full of clothes down to the river to be washed. We would light a fire on the riverbank, fill the bath with water and set it on the fire to boil. Maureen pummeled the clothes with a big stick until she was satisfied with their cleanliness. Then they were rinsed and hung on her makeshift line to dry. She was a resourceful woman.

At night we would play cards or by the light of the lamp read whatever books we could get hold of. At the end of the day when you went to bed you fell asleep instantly. I can still remember waking up and looking out the window at the stone walls—the beautiful stone walls with bits of lichen growing in them. It was a beautiful place.

The Shimna River, big and fast, flowed just below the house. We used to watch the salmon come up to spawn, jumping up the salmon leap, or 'salmon lep' as it was pronounced locally. Alan was good at poaching. I saw him take a salmon out of the river with a piece of copper wire, sliding the wire over its tail. Now that *is* a skill because a salmon's tail is always moving.

Billy loved trees and birds and was exceptionally knowledgeable about nature. Alan took after him. There wasn't a bird or a tree he couldn't identify.

We had an idyllic childhood. We climbed every fucking mountain in the Mournes. We used to call them Billy's Death Marches. When Billy took us out for the day, it literally meant the *whole* day.

There came a time when as teenagers you don't want to go and spend your holidays poaching and gutting salmon, lugging buckets of water and picking hazel nuts. We had the house into the 1960s. Alan took it for a while until he got a little house of his own, halfway up a mountain. When he and his wife Mary retired they bought a wee farm and an old farmhouse not far from Tullaree. They live there now and most of their children live near them in that part of County Down. Their eldest son, Liam, lives with them and helps with the garden and the hens.

Poster of International Brigades

In our street we were seen as 'other' and felt 'other' and I did not mind that. I liked the sense of difference.

I remember my father and me and my younger brother glued to radio reports about the Cuban Revolution. We were also aware of the history of the Spanish Civil War. Billy had supported the International Brigades. I still have a poster commemorating the International Brigades in my living room, in memory of him. He knew the veteran communist Mick O'Riordan, who fought in the Spanish Civil War, but Billy was more connected with the English internationalist movement in support of Republican Spain.

We talked constantly of politics, but never about Ireland. It was all about Russia, China, Cuba—liberation struggles and revolutions in other countries. Is communism viable? Can you have a communist regime in the modern world? These were common conversations, but there was never any conversation about Ireland. So, we were not a republican household. At least, not in the Irish sense. I remember my younger brother and I saying to my father, 'You know, Billy, we know about every liberation struggle in the world except our own.' And I remember him looking at us because it had never occurred to him. It just shows you what partition did to people who were from a Protestant background. Remember, he didn't consider himself a 'Prod' but an atheist. But people from that background with Billy's left-wing political views oriented towards Britain and the left there, and tended to take their lead from there rather than where they lived. His politics did not include a look at what colonialism had done to the country he was born in, the country he actually lived in. He didn't know any of it. He hadn't connected that Ireland was their first experiment at colonisation—the crushing of the language, rubbishing a people's culture and religion, rubbishing everything, making people feel they were inferior. They did a bloody good job of that.

Billy's father and mother were both dead by the time he was seventeen so he went to live with his older sister, who was the loveliest person you could meet. They were the ones in his family we would have known best.

If there is one reason alone why I remember the Twelfth in Belfast it was because my Da would have absolutely nothing to do with it. Detested it.

CHAPTER TWO

THE SIXTIES

I got married very young, at seventeen, at the end of 1960. I had met Gerry O'Hare when I got a summer job in Hughes Bakery where he was then working. We moved to England but came back to Belfast after a couple of years when our first child Terry was born. We had managed to save enough for a deposit on a house in Ladybrook, Andersonstown. I was very aware of current politics but I was too busy having babies to play any active role. Rory wasn't yet born, but the other two, Terry and Frances, were small. Gerry's family had republican connections. An uncle on his mother's side was an IRA veteran, Jimmy Steele, who escaped from Crumlin Road Prison in 1943, and whom I got to know. I began to realise that there was this whole history that I had never been taught, a *republican* account of partition and what it really meant.

I consciously chose to send my own children to Catholic schools because the alternative was a unionist school—an Orange school, to be frank. I actually sent Rory for a year to a wee school quite near us called Finaghy Primary and the first thing you saw when you walked in the door was a Union Jack and a picture of the English Queen on the wall. You didn't hear a word of Irish. You didn't hear anything about your own country. Everything was about England. Everything was through an English, unionist prism. Nobody said anything untoward to him; at least, not that I know of. If they had he would have been unaware of it. But he was marked out by his name. Picking a school was not about faith. It was a matter of identity. To be completely blunt, integrated education was one of the cleverest propaganda coups ever pulled off, because, as I discovered later, they had people in America believing that if Protestant and Catholic children were educated together everything would be solved. I stopped getting into rows with people about it because I could see that they couldn't understand. (I remember asking one of these big groups of rich people who were funding an integrated school, 'What school do your children go to? Do they go to the local state public school?' And they didn't! They went to a private Catholic school.)

Rita with baby Terry in pram

Alan, Rita, Bill, Billy holding Frances, Maureen, Terry, Norfolk Drive

The association between school and identity would become even stronger as resistance to the Brits and resistance to the unionist grip on the North became stronger. The Brits would push the line that the conflict was about Catholics and Protestants hating each other and that the Brits were there to try to keep us apart. We even made the same mistake, talking about Catholics against Protestants. It was never about Catholics or Protestants or religion. It was about *identity*, and it was about fear. If there was hatred, it was a hatred of people who were native Irish. It was the fear of the coloniser being overrun by the colonised.

In 1964, at the time of the general election, Sinn Féin was still a banned political party so it stood Billy McMillen as an independent republican for the West Belfast constituency. Their campaign headquarters was in Divis Street and they placed an Irish Tricolour in the window. It was there for weeks, unnoticed. But then Ian Paisley, who was then on the rise and had broken away to form his own Free Presbyterian Church, threatened to march 10,000 loyalists into the Falls district unless the RUC removed the Tricolour. No one realised how dangerous he would become. His aim was to increase polarization, scare and motivate unionists in the election. Later that day about fifty RUC men arrived. The office door was smashed in and the flag seized. Protests erupted into riots, the biggest and most prolonged for almost thirty years. This was Paisley's emergence as a political figure and his blatant bigotry drew support from all shades of unionism. And, of course, in the election the unionist candidate took the West Belfast seat on the back of an anti-nationalist and anti-republican wave.

Paisley *started* those riots which led to many people being imprisoned—and many in the community becoming politicised, so his attempt to intimidate an entire community backfired. The protests were too widespread to just die out and I remember thinking when I saw the reaction of the people to these police raids that a line had been crossed and they weren't going to be so easily beaten off the streets or so easily crushed as in the past.

People knew well that it was a dangerous thing to raise your head and to protest. At that time, around the Twelfth of July, there were always attacks on nationalists, with windows being smashed in the Clonard area of Belfast by Mackies' workers as they made their way home from the factory, often assaulting locals who would end up hospitalised. It was presented as being the norm, just high spirits.

Two years later republicans in West Belfast organised a big march to celebrate the fiftieth anniversary of the 1916 Rising. Stormont responded by banning public transport into the city to make it difficult for people to attend. The B Specials were mobilised and set up checkpoints on roads as well. I remember standing with Gerry's brother, Seamus O'Hare, watching the parade. It was more out of curiosity. I had never been to any sort of republican event before. I remember thinking that it was muted and very solemn and very well organised.

The Falls paid for that Easter commemoration. Gusty Spence from the Shankill Road was a former British soldier. He had re-formed the Ulster Volunteer Force as an armed paramilitary organization. Their first victim was John Scullion in the Clonard area of the Falls, who was shot in May 1966 and died a few weeks later. The RUC denied that John Scullion had been shot and said he had been stabbed. People had heard the shots! His family had to have his body exhumed and the autopsy then proved he'd been assassinated. A few weeks later the gang killed two more people. In an attempt to petrol-bomb a Catholic-owned bar on the Shankill they set alight the house next door. Matilda Gould, a Protestant pensioner, later died from burns. In another gun attack Spence shot dead seventeen-year-old Peter Ward from the Falls as he

25

left the Malvern Arms Pub. Remember, there was no IRA and no Civil Rights Association. The NICRA would be formed the following year. The shootings were aimed at terrifying nationalists generally, but sent out a message, especially in ghetto areas, that you faced being randomly killed just for existing.

There had been campaigns around housing, discrimination, the refusal to build homes for Catholics, and there had been the Campaign for Social Justice, but what really brought the matter to a head and to international attention was the formation of the Northern Ireland Civil Rights Movement (NICRA) and the civil rights march in Duke Street in Derry in October 1968.

I'd been to the march from Coalisland to Dungannon in August which was made up of men and women, some of whom were pushing prams. The RUC banned the protest from entering Market Square because loyalists opposed to civil rights occupied it. That was the first time that I met Dolours Price. Dolours was involved in People's Democracy (PD), but I didn't know she was also in the IRA. Her father, Albert, was a veteran IRA man. Gerry had been involved with the Republican Labour Party and then with PD, formed by Queen's University students. It attracted a lot of support from young people, including republicans. I knew its leader Michael Farrell and I got to know Dolours.

In Duke Street in Derry the RUC baton-charged the marchers, which included local representatives and some British Labour MPs, and it was all caught on camera. The reality of it was quite shocking. Thursday, 5 October, 1968, is often dated as the rise of the nationalist community against second-class citizenship but there was a lot of activism already happening.

What I realise now is that people were very quietly, cleverly, for their own protection, starting to talk about something that could not easily be put down: protests within the law, demanding rights that were the norm in any democratic society. They were not talking about revolution or a united Ireland—what they were talking about was reform, they were talking about civil rights, rights that applied to 'British citizens' which unionists boasted almost non-stop we all were. Indeed, this mantra that we were British was rammed down our throats. I think there was a feeling and a commitment to see what could be got, what there was a basis for. The Gandhi philosophy was popular at the time: 'We will never use violence even though it is used against us.'

NICRA protested against the denial of basic human rights. Its demands were modest: equality in public housing allocation and jobs and the right to vote. The slogan, at the time, was 'One Man, One Vote!' When I think back about that chant it is embarrassing! I was also embarrassed by and later protested against the saying of the Rosary at republican commemorations which were supposed to be secular. I understood why it happened, because the republican tradition was carried on by people who were largely Catholic in faith and they kept the flame of republicanism lit. But the two should never be confused, should never be mistaken as being synonymous. I have never been happy with that. Reciting the Catholic Rosary at the grave of Wolfe Tone, born Church of Ireland! The same for Roger Casement.

It didn't take long for me to realise that you could march from here to China for civil rights and the only thing you were certain to get was a baton over your head. Peaceful protest wasn't going to succeed because unionists were not for giving even basic reforms. The whole language and rhetoric of unionists from partition was 'not an inch', 'what we have we hold', and 'we're a Protestant Parliament for a Protestant People.' Because the 'No Surrender' stance had always been successful and had maintained the status quo for almost fifty years, they were unlikely to abandon it willingly. Reform of the Orange State was impossible. It was so anti-democratic to begin with, its boundaries defined geographically by a sectarian headcount, perpetuated by policies of discrimination in housing and employment, and the denial of a voice to, and indeed the humiliation of, even those nationalists who periodically engaged with it. The unionist default position was always repression, the repression of those who disagreed and opposed it, even by non-violent means.

I was rearing my kids but I had the indulgence of being able to stand back and look and watch, although, as I said, I was at some of the marches. But I was coming around to the view that the civil rights movement, if it achieved anything, would only extract limited reforms. It was never going to change the *nature* of the state, never going to get rid of the state.

PD had quite a few 'Prods' among them. Some of us later worked together on *An Phoblacht/Republican News* when I was editor working out of Parnell Square. They included John McGuffin who also became a satirical writer for *Republican News* in his 'Brigadier' column and before that wrote the books *Internment* and *The Guinea Pigs* about 'the hooded men' and British torture.

I liked PD because it was left-wing and had an all-Ireland stance on rights. Both the Civil Rights Campaign and People's Democracy declared that they would not retaliate if attacked. And attacked they were, in full view of the RUC, who also frequently were the attackers. Three months later, the PD march from Belfast to Derry in January 1969 shocked people by the savagery of the violence used against the students along the route and the actions of the RUC. They were ambushed at Burntollet Bridge by about three hundred unionists, including B Specials, and driven into the river. The press was there and the images of the police joining in the attack on these young people, blood pouring from their heads, were transmitted around the world. It opened the eyes of many beyond the North about what life was like for us. One iconic photograph was of a young student, Billy Campbell, with blood streaming down his face after being struck by a baton. A battle had begun—a war. What nobody realised was that it would go on for so long.

The biggest impact of those images was in Ireland, particularly the six counties. And worse was to come.

I knew that equal rights were not going to be tolerated. Unionism might entertain some reform with a few wee frills but nothing substantial, nothing that would challenge the core sectarianism of the state, nothing that would give the 'native' Irish a real say, some control, some power. I viewed the situation in terms of colonialism which, of course, hadn't happened only in Ireland. Hadn't happened only in India. And the Brits weren't the only guilty imperial power. There were other colonisers. But the core of it was the same: divide and conquer; subjugate the native people, take their land, their language, take away their identity, keep them in fear, inferior, and impotent, otherwise they will rise up and take back their country and will *fuck* you out. Unionists were only following this golden, inflexible precept. Their sectarianism blinded them. A cleverer way to neutralize the nationalist community and its aspirations would have been to actually have made them feel welcome, have made them feel they had a stake in society. But in reality they looked down on nationalists as inferior and didn't want them in the state. You could see this through the practice of deliberate deprivation. All government policies around housing and employment favoured unionists, the 'loyal' citizens, and were aimed at driving out the 'Irish', and it worked for quite a time because the vast majority who emigrated were nationalists.

One thing the British and the unionist establishment could never do was to be truthful about the cause of the conflict, about the magnitude of the repression, about the first violence and the first civilian deaths all of which they were responsible for. The IRA, which was dormant, was blamed for the bombing campaign in 1969 which was actually carried out by loyalists to destabilise Terence O'Neill's government at Stormont and prevent reform.

There was trouble after the Apprentice Boys march in Derry in early August 1969. The RUC tried to get into the Bogside but the young people were determined to prevent them. This was because after a civil rights meeting in April the RUC had broken into the home of a man called Sammy Devenny and beat him with batons in front of his wife and children. He later died from his wounds. To this day the British government has maintained its 'conspiracy of silence' and refuses to release the classified files on his killing.

During what became known as the Battle of the Bogside we drove to Derry. Myself, Gerry O'Hare and others from PD in Gerry's minibus. By the time we got there it was very difficult to get near to where the action was taking place. I think we had to walk quite a bit because of closed roads and traffic being stopped. It was my first time in Derry. I remember seeing people making petrol bombs openly on the streets. Eventually, we managed to get in behind the barricades. There were a lot of people coming in from outside to support the frontline at Rossville Flats. Kids on top of the flats had raised the Tricolour. The Northern state was on one side, northern nationalists on the other.

Things were very well organised: there was a production line set up to make petrol bombs. Martina Anderson sent me a photograph recently of her making petrol bombs during the Battle of the Bogside with other women. And that's what I saw that day. When I read Eamonn McCann's *War and an Irish Town* it brought it all back, the days of Free Derry. Families gave their houses over for people to eat and sleep in. McCann wrote about the everlasting stew. How everybody didn't get food poisoning, I will never know! McCann and Bernadette Devlin were terrific speakers with great politics. I was aware of Bernadette when I went to Derry because of her involvement with PD. Later, she would stay with us in Dublin.

Later that week, in Belfast, the nationalist community paid the price for Derry's victory over the RUC.

Unionists like to think it all started in 1969.

It didn't.

There had been pogroms in the North in the immediate aftermath of partition that aimed at driving out all non-unionists, that is those with an Irish identity. Mobs rampaging through areas and setting fire to houses, whole streets being burned and Catholics murdered or driven out. Pogroms against Catholics were happening before 1969. My mother, when she was about twelve or thirteen, was coming home from a piano lesson. She saw what she thought was a dog lying in the street and imagined it had been knocked down. But then she realised it was a man and ran home to tell her mother. Her parents reported it and my mother was to make a statement to the RUC. The man was a Catholic who had been shot down on the street and was lying there, dying from his wounds. The police never took a statement and there was no investigation. My father, when he was eleven, saw mobs coming over the waste ground near his home in East Belfast. They were coming to burn a Catholic family, the Clarkes, out of their house at the top of Rosebery Road. The Clarkes owned several houses in the area and the McCullochs rented theirs from them. My grandfather and Billy's older brothers went up the alley, got the family out and brought them to their home for safety.

The British Army arrived on our streets in August 1969 at the request of then Stormont Prime Minister Major Chichester-Clark. The myth that it was there to defend Catholic areas from attack by loyalists was quickly dispelled. Nationalist Coates Street, in the shadow of Hastings Street Barracks down the Falls, was attacked that October and burned down by loyalists whilst the British Army and RUC stood watching. The frequency of British Army confrontations with nationalist youths in Derry and Ballymurphy, the number of growing raids and searches in our areas, was a pointer as to where this was going.

In June 1970 the Catholic Church of St Matthew's in Ballymacarrett, where my mother grew up, was attacked. It was the IRA not the British Army which defended the area. The following weekend the British Army surrounded the Falls, declared a curfew (which turned out to be illegal), came in firing, saturated the streets and small homes with choking CS gas, killed five civilians and wounded many more.

All through the existence of the Northern state, nationalists were being put down, humiliated, denied day and daily the rights that people in the South, people in England, were entitled to, enjoyed and took for granted.

Nobody in the Irish Establishment said a fucking word about this until the people in nationalist working-class and poor rural areas rose up and fought back through the IRA, however ably or imperfectly. Only then did Dublin governments—which derived their independence from the Tan War which they commemorated, if not glorified—found their voice. They then had plenty to say by means of condemnation, and slander and distorting the truth. The hypocrites. They worked hand-in-hand with British governments and were effectively endorsing the status quo, comforting the British in their pursuit of Irish republicans and perpetuating the conflict by postponing meaningful, *all*-party talks.

There comes a point of asking yourself are *you* going to do anything about what is happening or are you going to keep quiet. It becomes frighteningly personal. Is marching and demanding civil rights ever going to get anything or get us anywhere. It wasn't just me who faced it or had to tackle it. Stand up now or you never will. It was one of those now or never moments. You let one more thing go—if another line is crossed and you let it go—you'll never stand up. It is a hard, tough, personal decision with implications for you and your immediate family. Every person who found themselves in these circumstances had to consider whether to go down the road of physical force, of the IRA. It was a dilemma, an anguish, similarly, universally, faced by many people of good conscience in many lands, many times, across history. For some people it was a hard decision; for others, an easy one. I would never criticise anyone who balked at fighting, particularly on moral grounds. But I would go on to resent those politicians and clerics who lived *above* the Troubles and who for their own agendas misrepresented and slandered our sacrifices and the struggle to end British rule in Ireland.

After the August pogroms in 1969 I had learnt of the increasing upheaval within the Republican Movement and the rancour at the failure of its leadership, despite repeated warnings, to properly prepare for the defence of nationalist areas. Jimmy Steele, Billy McMillan and Billy McKee and Máire Drumm were big figures in Belfast at the time and made their views clear.

When the Goulding faction split, becoming known as 'the Officials', there was some attempt to portray it as a split between socialists and nationalists. Now, there was some basis for this, considering some of the personalities involved, but overall it was a facile depiction. The priority in 1969 and 1970 was in building an organisation that could defend vulnerable nationalist areas, not in lauding Russia as an exemplar state, and orienting the Republican Movement slavishly towards the USSR and the Warsaw Pact countries.

Cathal Goulding's denigration of the struggle for national independence as a sectarian pursuit, or one that could wait until an elusive workers' unity was achieved in the North, took many of his supporters down a blind alley to such an extent that today the final incarnation of his organisation, the Workers Party, is practically non-existent.

Coming from a household with a very left-wing, internationalist perspective, it might have been expected that my sense of republicanism would have been more inclined towards the Goulding faction, and not towards those the media pejoratively referred to as 'the Provisionals'. And indeed some of them did try to woo me. I didn't personally know Goulding or any of the Southern leadership. But I knew some of the local leadership and I had a lot of respect for their acumen and political nous. What I knew also was that the proposition of doing a wee bit of fighting, just to keep some people quiet, which was what they did, and losing some courageous young people in the process, was cynical and was not going to work.

It was clear to me that the aim of the Goulding faction was to establish a political party, based largely in and managed in the South. And I knew that this was never going to meaningfully address the colonial situation we found ourselves in the North. From my knowledge of other countries' colonial experiences, particularly involving Brits, colonists never give anything up until they are forced to. The Brits were never going to suddenly feel guilty about their horrendous treatment and murder of innocents in half of the world. Their heroes? People like Cecil Rhodes who in one afternoon presided over the murder of thousands of native people in Africa because there were diamonds on their land. His forces used new Maxim machineguns against poor people armed with spears and he gave the order to just mow them down.

CHAPTER THREE

TO PRISON

'We will be back before the kids come home from school.'

I have reminded Margaret Gatt of her words many times during the fifty years since she asked me to join her and other women at a protest one Friday morning in February 1971.

The two of us were friends since we moved in next door to each other in Andersonstown in the early 1960s. Margaret had two children then, Karen and Mike (and Carmen in 1973); and I had three, Terry, Frances and Rory. They were all at primary school. Margaret said she was going to a protest at the Courts in Belfast with some other women and did I want to go.

Several young men were about to be sentenced that day for taking part in the funeral of James Saunders, a member of the IRA, who had been shot and killed by the British Army during a gun battle in the Oldpark area of Belfast. The charges against them would carry an automatic mandatory six months' imprisonment as a result of a new law passed by unionists at Stormont aimed exclusively at republicans. It covered charges ranging from rioting to wearing 'paramilitary' clothing, to carrying an offensive weapon.

A combat jacket was deemed to be paramilitary clothing and a hurl, or hurling stick used in Gaelic sport, was deemed an 'offensive' weapon. The men had worn combat jackets—British Army surplus coats that were worn by students and people with little money. I had one myself: they were warm, waterproof and very cheap. The men had carried hurls at the Saunders' funeral to protect mourners from attack by loyalists, which had happened just earlier at the funeral of Bernard Watt, a civilian killed by the British Army.

The situation in Belfast had been deteriorating daily since the attacks on the peaceful Civil Rights marches across the North beginning in 1968. Whole streets in Catholic areas of Belfast had been burnt down by loyalists in August 1969, acting often with the backing of the RUC and B Specials. All the demonstrations of opposition to the sectarianism of the state, the publicity campaigns, the agitation, the appeals for reform, had been unsuccessful and no real redress was forthcoming. Armed resistance was the inevitable consequence.

I agreed to go with Margaret. After all, it was a peaceful protest against a discriminatory law. However, we were arrested within minutes of arriving at the courthouse and were charged with wearing paramilitary clothing. We were sentenced to six months' imprisonment. I still wonder at the sheer stupidity of this decision to prosecute as it galvanised support for anyone convicted under this law, particularly women. It was later repealed, but *after* we had served our sentences.

Despite it being a seminal moment in my life, I can't remember how we were transported to Armagh. I just remember arriving there and being brought to the basement where our clothes and possessions were taken from us. There then followed the compulsory bath and being given a prison uniform. I do remember laughing at the sight of Margaret, who was always very elegant, dressed in the truly ugly prison-uniform brown skirt. It would be some time later, when prisoners became better organised, when militancy was buoyed by the rising number of new inmates, that an issue was made of the degrading and humiliating prison uniform and the government was forced to allow female prisoners to wear their own clothes.

The prison was old, built at the time of the Famine, and was like something you would see in old movies: tiers of cells laid out around a circle, iron stairs accessing each tier. All the cells were the same: a barred window high on the wall facing the heavy sheeted door with the spyhole. Iron bedstead, horsehair mattress and a pillow that must have dated from the nineteenth century and hard as a rock. A locker and a chamber pot completed the museum piece.

There were already some political prisoners in Armagh when we arrived, and we were to be quickly joined by others as the struggle escalated. It was clear to me that the prison administration was not at all prepared for women activists, as if it had never occurred to the regime that women would be involved in struggle.

For any of us with children our main concern was for them. The hardest thing was visits as we were not allowed to touch them and a screw sat at the table beside us, monitoring our conversation. The great consolation for me was that my mother moved into our house in Ladybrook in Andersonstown and looked after the children.

Armagh Prison. Photo: Rab Kerr

Of the women already in the prison, Anne Maguire stands out in my memory, her long red hair swinging in a ponytail. She too had small children, as had several others. I am in touch with Anne still. Mary McGuigan from Ardoyne was there and other women I would get to know well. There were three generations of republicans in Armagh at the time: grandmothers, mothers, daughters. Some of the older women were veterans who had been involved in resistance to the Orange State all their adult lives and had been imprisoned before. I met women who were able, clever, articulate. I was very conscious of how they lived, where they lived and the sectarianism that dominated their lives. The younger women were equally capable, but because they were Catholics they had been denied opportunities to progress and develop and prosper. It was then that I realised that sectarianism was not just some academic study. Here were examples of it, of people whose mothers and fathers before them were denied the ability to live the sort of full lives they should have, had they not been subjugated by this sectarian state.

Here to me was the classic example of the colonialism and colonisation that we had talked about at home, when it was Africa or India, and it was right on my doorstep. It was on my fucking doorstep.

Most of the screws seemed utterly bemused by us. Some of them were born-again Christians who were there, they told us, to help us mend our ways. I remember one of us found out that we were entitled to a daily piece of fruit. The screws hadn't been used to prisoners demanding their rights, even to an apple a day, and this was seen as a great victory.

At home I had been in the middle of exams and to my surprise the governor agreed to accommodate my studies and sitting the finals. I received my textbooks, and my tutor was allowed to visit a few times. I was concerned that the other prisoners would resent this, but I never heard anyone express anything but encouragement.

Prison work was mainly keeping the place clean. I studied a few hours every day and sat the exams sometime in June. Later, I found out that I got very high marks and the governor considered it a great feather in his cap that one of 'his' prisoners had passed!

I have a memory of a film being shown an odd time and there was a recreation room. I can't remember if there was a TV but there was a radio, and we did manage to get news about the growing tension on the outside, the house-to-house searches by the British Army, the almost daily shootings.

Other changes were happening. Decimal currency was introduced, and they brought people in to explain it to us and show us what money now looked like, the old ten-shilling note replaced by a seven-sided 50p coin.

Margaret and I were released in July.

I would not be at large for long.

CHAPTER FOUR

SHOT

My husband Gerry, the three kids and I, went to Donegal for a little family holiday in the summer of 1971. We were there when internment was brought in, used exclusively against nationalists and republicans. In Ballymurphy the Paratroopers had massacred eleven civilians on the 9, 10 and 11 of August, including the local priest, Fr Hugh Mullan, killed while waving a white cloth as he went to the aid of a wounded man, and mother-of-eight, Joan Connolly. Among the wounded were brothers Martin Butler, aged nine, and Edward, aged eleven. That same regiment would carry out the Bloody Sunday massacre in Derry five months later.

From Donegal I telephoned a neighbour for news and she told me that the Brits and the RUC had broken into our house and wrecked it. It was Gerry O'Hare they were looking for.

There was the loveliest family, the Shields, who lived near where we were on the Fanad Peninsula, and they wanted to keep Rory. 'Leave him with us, he is so young. We will look after him.' However, we couldn't do that, couldn't break up the family. How ironic.

We returned to Belfast. I remember being so angry at the wanton destruction in the house and the theft of my grandmother's silver spoons that I rang British Army Headquarters in Lisburn to complain. A woman answered the phone and jeered and laughed at me. I remember saying to her before I hung up, 'You will be laughing on the other side of your face before this is over.'

In Belfast you had to have some sort of normal life because of the children but this was not normality. There was an uprising already raging that could not be put down.

Gerry was staying away from the house but a few weeks later he came back to get some clothes and the Brits and the RUC swooped and caught him. Someone local must have informed. The kids were very upset, scared and crying. He was taken first to Crumlin Road Jail. I was able to visit him after about a week. Most of the visitors were women. The women were the stalwarts during all those years. They were the visitors, the supporters, the providers, the organisers of protests, all while keeping families together and cared for.

There were daily battles in Belfast, and it got closer. You could hear gunfire and sirens. There were no-go areas in many of the estates in Andersonstown with barricades to stop the Brits getting in or to slow down their attempts and give people the opportunity to escape. There wasn't open armed combat on the street where we lived, but you could hear it—the sounds of battle in the housing estates. The riots after the Ballymurphy massacre and the protests about internment continued. Heavy raids and searches were now a daily and nightly feature of life.

I had joined the IRA, first with A Company in Andersonstown, then F Company, also in the First Battalion of the Belfast Brigade.

In the early hours of 23 October, a Saturday, soldiers from the Royal Green Jackets regiment were sent into the Falls, occupying Cape Street and Leeson Street.

Dorothy Maguire and her sister Maura Meehan and two other people started to drive through the streets warning that the soldiers had got into the district and were raiding. The two sisters were in the back seat and were using a bullhorn to raise the alarm. Without warning, they were both shot dead. Maura was thirty and married with four children. Dorothy was nineteen. The shock and anger at their killing added to the tension and fear people were living with.

That Sunday night during a bombing operation in the city centre an IRA Volunteer, Martin Forsyth, from our First Battalion, was shot dead and a female comrade was badly wounded, which resulted in her being paralysed for life.

It was during the British Army operation to take control of streets in Andersonstown a few hours later that I was shot.

Editor's note

When news about the death of Martin Forsyth and the wounding of his comrade reached the IRA it realized that the homes of both Volunteers would be raided. The search of Martin Forsyth's had already commenced but in the Rosnareen area the IRA rushed around thirteen armed Volunteers to cover the four main entries to the estate. To gain stealth the British Army cut through the back fence of St Mary's Grammar School so that their Saracens could silently freewheel down to the Glen Road from the Upper Springfield Road and to the entrance of Ramoan Gardens. However, the IRA was monitoring the radio traffic between the various British Army units, was expecting the soldiers and immediately engaged them. A small directional mine hastily placed at the entrance to Greenan, about half a mile away, seems to have only partially exploded.

In 2023 Ciaran Mac Airt, of the Belfast-based charity, Paper Trail (Legacy Archive Research), located the British Army's Log Sheets for the soldiers of the 25 Light Regiment involved in Rita's shooting, which happened around 5 am.

The British Army had been fired on in numerous locations in West Belfast: three times from Ardmonagh Gardens—at 0335 (15-20 shots), at 0400 (8-10 burst of fire from a light machine gun) and 0435 (100 rounds from a light machine gun); from Divis Drive to Andersonstown Barracks at 0435 (20 rounds in three bursts of automatic fire; followed by four single shots); and 0440 and 0445, respectively, single shots from Beechmount Avenue and Locan Street. They were also shot at in Andersonstown Park West; there were two bomb scares in the Whiterock and Springfield Road areas; and the logs state that one of their ambulances came under fire at the junction of Glen Crescent and the Falls Road and, bizarrely, '3 x SMG returned by doctor'—that is, the doctor fired back with a submachine gun. Their initial report describes Rita as a civilian caught in crossfire, 'VSI' [very seriously injured]. In another paragraph they report sporadic firing from 0500 until 0535 from the back of Kenard Avenue and Ramoan Gardens; that fire is returned; and that a Battery Sergeant Major was shot with a pistol from ten yards and received a wound to his arm. 'Another soldr [soldier] shot the shooter from other side of house. This was [REDACTED]. She was treated for head and shoulder GSW [gunshot wounds]. Had trousers on. When they returned for wpn [weapon], NTR [Nothing To Report].'

In another report at 0640 they describe Rita as 'Well known.' The next log goes into a bit more detail about the incident and says that they broke into two parties to approach the Ramoan/Kenard area from the north and the south. Three to four nail bombs were thrown at the north-approach group and they were sniped at in Ramoan Gardens. The south-approach group were met by a minor explosion and they were 'then fired on from both sides of Greenan immediately prior to turning into Tullymore Gardens. 17 x 7.62 fired in reply. No cas [casualties]. At 0510 HRS in Kenard Avenue soldier moved around side of brick outhouse in area [REDACTED] to be confronted by two figures about 10 metres away. One crouched pointing gun at him about two single shots were fired one wounding him. At the same time one soldier came round other side of building returned the fire one figure fell ... Wounded civilian shot in abdomen and further injured head on falling. Taken to RVH. She was dressed in jeans and dark clothing.'

On the way to hospital I lost consciousness and the next thing I remember, after being in theatre for several hours, was waking up in a secure ward and who is standing there but Billy, my beautiful Da. He was holding my hand. I was still under the effects of general anaesthetic and lost consciousness again. When I came round, I was guarded by two British soldiers, one outside the door and one inside the room.

I had been shot several times. Once in the back, in the hip, and the bullet had travelled up as far as my ribcage and then down again and exited at my pelvis, ripping through me. These wounds were inflicted by a bullet from a British Army SLR, a high velocity Self-Loading Rifle. I had severe internal injuries to my bowel, intestines and pelvic area as well as nerve damage in my hip but no main organs were damaged and the bullet missed my spine as well.

The other shots came from a Sterling submachine gun and they had gone through my shoulder before hitting my head. The fact that they were ricochets diminished their impact. I was shot in the fucking head and still recovered.

People think when you get hit in the head that's it—but while it caused a bleed in the brain, it was the internal injuries that nearly killed me. They were more serious.

AGE 3 RBDA88 009 R E S T R I C T E D

████████████████████████████████████. THESE THREE WERE CLOSELY
QUESTIONED, GAVE CONFLICTINR STORIES AND WERE SENT O HOLYWOOD.
. 3. DURING SEARCHES FOLLOWINR SHOOTING INCIDENTS:
  A. AT 0335 WHITEROCK GRAVE YARD, 15-20 RDS AUTO AT PL FROM
     ARDMONAGH GDNS. NIL CAS. NFR.
  B. AT 0400 WHITEROCK CHALETS, 8-10 BURST OF LMG AT PTL FROM
     ARDMONAGH GDNS. NIL CAS, NFD.
  C. AT 0435 WHITEROCK CHALETS BURSTS OF LMG FROM ARDMONAGH GDNS
     NIL CAS 3 X 7.62 RETURNED. APPROX TOTAL OF 100 RDS FIRED AT
     SF.
  D. SHOTS AT V28 IN CAVENDISH ST:
     (1) 0440 1 X SINGLE SHOT FROM BEECHMOUNT AVE NO CAS NTR.
     (2) 0445 1 X SINGLE SHOT FROM LOCON ST. NIL CAS. NTR.
 TWO PD SHOOTING INCIDENTS 0430-0530 25 OCT. 25 LT PD
   1. A. 0435 20 RDS IN 3 BURSTS OF AUTOMATIC FIRE AT TPS AT TOP
        END DIVIS DRIVE BUS STATION. FROM AREA FALLS PARK. 9X7.62
        RETURNED ONE CAS ████████████ FLESH WOUND IN BUTTOCK NOW
        IN MUSGRAVE PARK HSPL.
ANDERSONSTOWN 4 SINGLE SHOTS AT SANGAR RUC STATI

AGE 4 RBDA88 009 R E S T R I C T E D
 AREA WIERTOWN CEMETERY. 5 X 7.62 RETURNED BY SENTRY. NO
      CASJM
      C. 0515 5 RDS AT MIL AMBULANCE 200 METRES FROM RUC STATION
      ANDERSONSTOWN SOUTH DOWN FALLS ROAD FROM AREA OF RUINED
      GARAGE. 3 X SMG RETURNED. NO CAS.
   2. EVENTS CONNECTED WITH SEARCH OF ████████████ (NTR).
      0445 SOUND OF 3-4 NAIL BOMBS HEARD IN ROSSNAREEN AREA ON
      APPROACH.
      0500 A. NORTH APPROACH GROUP SNIPED AT IN ROMOAN GDNS. NO
           FIRE RETURNED NO CAS.
           B. SOUTH APPROACH GROUP MET BY MINOR EXPLOSION
           APPEARED TO BE DETONATED NO DAMAGE. NO CAS. THIS GROUP
           THEN FIRED ON FROM BOTH SIDES OF GREENAN IMMEDIATELY
           PRIOR TO TURNING INTO TULLYMORE GDNS. 17 X 7.62 FIRED
           IN REPLY. NO CAS
           C. 0510 HRS IN KENARD AVE. SOLDIER MOVED AROUND SIDE O
           BRICK OUTHOUSE IN AREA ████████████ TO BE CONFRONTED
           BY TWO FIGURES ABOUT 10 METRES AWAY. ONE CROUCHED POIN
           -TING GUN AT HIM ABOUT TWO SINGLE SHOTS WERE FIRED ONE
           WOUNDING HIM. AT HE SAME TIME ONE SOLDIER CAME ROUND

AGE 5 RBDA88 009 R E S T R I C T E D
           OTHER SIDE OF BLDG RETURNED THE FIRE ONE FIGURE FELL
HER RAN AWAY ANDINBSDAPEBESOUTH INTO
           ROMOAN GDS VIA FOOTPAH WOUNDED CIVILIAN SHOT IN ABDOME
           AND FURTHER INJURED HEAD ON FALLING. TAKEN TO RVH. SHE
           WAS DRESSED IN JEANS AND DARK CLOTHINGS AND IS ████████
           OF ████████████. MIL CAS IS ████████
           GSW THROUGH RICEP NOW IN MUSGRAVE PK HOSPITAL.
 THREE PD 0350 1 GH PD 20/30 MEN PTL WOMEN STONED AND BOTTLED A
    PIG JUNCT NORTHWICK/ETNA. 6 X BAT RDS FIRED. SIT SOON NORMAL.
 FOUR PD 0750 25 LT PD 0750 PARCEL BOMB REPORTED TO RUC OUTSIDE
    ████████████ NOT INVESTIGATED. AT 0815 3 MEN REMOVED PARCEL
 AND DROVE OFF IN CAR.
 FIVE PD 1025 RMP PD ARMED ROBBERY: ████████████████████
    YORK LANEJM ARMED MAN WENT TO REAR DOOR, HELD UP MANAGER OF PA
    POUNDS 850 STOLEN FROM SAFE. MAN ESCAPED IN CAR. NO DETAILS
    KNOWN.
 SIX PD 1245 25 LT PD 4 MEN TOLD OWNER OF ████████████
    ████████████, BELIEVED POSSIBLE INTIMIDATION.
 SEVEN PD 1245 25 LT PD 4 ARMED MEN ENTERED JUSTICE ████████
    ████████████. ONLY COOK (FEMALE) PRESENT. ████

This British Army ammunition box, and two others, for a general-purpose machine gun were left behind in the Rosnareen area at the time of the gun battle when Rita was shot. Courtesy: Roddy McCorley Museum, donated by John O'Carroll. Photograph: Peadar Whelan.

The head surgeon in the Royal at the time was John Robb. He came to see me after I had been operated on. He was a good man and became politically active in the New Ireland Group and wrote extensively about his views on peace and reconciliation from his Presbyterian and unionist background. He asked me if I had been treated well, which I was. I remember word for word what another surgeon who operated on me said. He brought students in and told them: 'You better see this one because you are going to have to get used to dealing with stuff like this.'

This doctor later told me: 'I've seen people who had one of the wounds you have, and you have several, particularly internal injuries. I've seen people with one of the hits that you took who have died, you have survived this.' And he added, 'You should go down on your knees to your mother because you were clearly very well nourished and looked after.'

I had a strong constitution and good genes, and I was young and fit.

I was in the RVH for a couple of weeks. I healed quickly. Billy came to see me every day. My mother had once again moved into our house in Ladybrook to look after the children. She found it too hard to see me in hospital, to visit, so I decided to write her a little note. I was shocked when I could not write, that what was in my brain would not convey instructions to my hand. I could not read either. That lasted till the swelling in my brain went down.

Billy brought the kids to see me. He felt they needed to see that I was going to be okay. Though my head was still bandaged the bruising and swelling on my face had receded. The children were unbelievable, just wanted to know when I would be home.

The young soldier who was on duty in the room that day gave them half a crown each and got the one outside to get them Coca-Cola. Those acts of kindness and humanity from the young soldier in the PIG and then from this young soldier demonstrated to me that many of them were not thugs but young men who joined the British Army for a job or the experience and did not expect to be in the middle of a conflict they knew nothing about. My time in Musgrave would bear that out.

As soon as I was well enough to be moved the RUC came in and charged me with the attempted murder of a soldier who had been injured that night in Andersonstown.

I was shot in the early hours of 25 October and I was in the Royal into November. I can't remember how long I was in Musgrave. It seems to me that I was in Musgrave longer but that could be because I was awake and conscious when I was there.

In Musgrave Military Wing they put me in a small ward off a big ward which was full of wounded soldiers, including Fraser Paton, the soldier shot that night in Andersonstown, though we never spoke or interacted. The nurses were all military as well.

It was utterly bizarre because all these wee soldiers were coming in and asking me could I get them hankies and souvenirs from republican prisoners in the Kesh and asking me to sign things for them. I said no, of course, but I did talk to them. A few of them told me that some of the others had 'shot themselves to get off the streets'. Another told me: 'We don't know what we are doing here.' A lot of them were from the traditionally poorer north of England. They hadn't a fucking clue about what was going on in Ireland. And they weren't all thugs; they were afraid. They were turned by circumstances and consequences into the thugs you then saw on the street. I felt sorry for a lot of them.

I was taken from Musgrave to appear in court, though I was not well enough. I was taken to the court in Belfast by car and locked in a cell until appearing. I was on crutches as I had nerve damage in my left leg from the shooting. I was brought from the cell into a corridor under the court where other prisoners, all male, were waiting. I recognised one of them, from the well-known McGuigan family from Ardoyne. They were sitting along the wall on either side on rows of chairs. As I was brought in and down the corridor, one of them called out to the others and they all stood up as I walked through them as if I was some dignitary. That is something I will never forget. The comradeship. I had to stand in the dock and was asked who was representing me. I was about to say no one when a man jumped up from the well of the court and said, 'I am. I am representing this woman.' So, I had a solicitor. It was Paddy McGrory, or 'PJ' as he was affectionately known. I was taken back to Musgrave but after a week I was moved again, back to Armagh Jail which I had left only four months earlier.

Armagh was now a political prison—and those screws who worked there knew that everything had changed. Internment, the British Army carnage of internment week, the torturing of what became known as 'the hooded men', had crossed the line. They knew it and the Irish Government knew it, but of course did nothing. The anger, the growth in resistance, was not something that could be suppressed quickly or easily. The 'explosion' had been long in the making—fifty years of humiliation and discrimination the immediate experience for generations of nationalists.

I was in a cell on the lower tier, with remand prisoners. Before, one of the worst things had been the beds with their horsehair mattresses and pillows like granite. They must have been there from when the jail was built. Have you ever slept on a horsehair mattress—it's not what you'd call comfy. But these cells now had beds with an ordinary mattress and pillow. I could not have lain on a horsehair pillow with the wound in my head which was still very raw and open. They were very careful around me—they didn't want me to get an infection or for anything to happen on their watch. They didn't want to generate protests either inside or outside the prison. It wasn't 'the milk of human kindness' so much as not wanting trouble. I didn't have visits but they couldn't stop me from seeing other prisoners who were awaiting trial. I remember Máire Drumm who'd been on remand just before we got out in July, but on a different wing. She managed to get to see me. Another remand was Brenda Murphy who later became a very successful writer and playwright. She would help me to the bathroom and help me get a bath. I preferred her and other republican women doing it rather than one of the screws.

There was a second court appearance and afterwards I had to wait a long time for transport. I was totally exhausted. When I got back to Armagh I could barely get out of the car. The prison doctor was called and was concerned enough that he got in touch with the Royal and a surgeon came to see me a few days later.

My next appearance was on the 23 December, and the wonderful Paddy McGrory made an application for bail. The crown prosecutor objected and said they could link me to the shooting. We were of the view that charging me was more to do with creating a public perception that women were active in the IRA and trying to justify their killing of Maura Meehan and Dorothy Maguire. I remember one soldier giving evidence and saying it was a very bright, clear night—which it wasn't. He said there was a full moon and he could see me clearly. That was a lie. There was no full moon.

PJ stood up and simply undermined the so-called testimony.

'Where is the hard evidence here at all? There is none.'

And it was on that basis that I got bail.

I was stunned. Stunned and relieved. It was very close to Christmas. Gerry's older brother, Seamus, put up the principal bail of £2000 for me and there were two other sureties of £1000 each.

While at home recovering we were asked if we agreed to be interviewed by Marcel Ophüls for his documentary about the Troubles, *A Sense of Loss.* He and his crew spent some hours at our home with us and the kids.

After another remand hearing in early January 1972 young soldiers in the hallway, some of whom had made statements against me, showed their anger and hatred. One of them said, 'That bitch is going to get off. I should have finished her off when I had her. But there will be other chances to get her, or her children.' A lot of people heard him. We made a complaint to the Registrar of the Court but nothing was done, no heed was taken. I think I realised then that I could not stay in Belfast—my life was clearly under threat.

45

CHAPTER FIVE

MOVING TO DUBLIN

It was a wrench for me and the children having to leave our home, their friends, our dear neighbours, leaving my elderly mother and father, leaving Belfast, a city I loved. Terry was nine, Frances was seven and Rory was five.
I would never see Belfast again.

We didn't sell the house in Ladybrook, thinking we would be back in a couple of years. We felt that exposure of the scandalous treatment of the nationalist community under partition would result in pressure from the Irish Government, the international community and the Irish around the world, and would put Britain so much under the spotlight that sooner rather than later there would be a political solution and settlement. Nobody thought the Troubles would last more than two or three years.

We counted without the disgraceful behavior of Irish governments whose real interest and priority throughout—it became ever more clear—was the protection of the twenty-six-county state which fixed the boundary 'of the march of a nation', to paraphrase Parnell.

In Belfast my husband Gerry was then rearrested and interned in Long Kesh again until March 1973.

Though I hadn't been in Dublin long and was still getting settled I attended most of the republican press conferences and got to know Ruairí Ó Brádaigh and Dave O'Connell. Joe Cahill was also prominent, having escaped Belfast during the introduction of internment and given an IRA press conference in Ballymurphy, rejecting claims that the IRA had been badly damaged by the arrests.

Joe was the oldest republican around then, from the 1940s, but Ruairí and Dave had been involved in the 1950s and had served many terms of imprisonment and suffered many privations for the republican cause. They were very dedicated patriots and although I later disagreed with them when they left Sinn Féin in 1986 over the issue of abstentionism, the truth is that over decades they worked against impossible odds to defend the struggle and establish a political foothold for Sinn Féin, and they were viciously demonised and slandered by the British and Irish media.

Let's remember that people like Ruairí and Dave 'kept the flame' alive.

But for a variety of reasons they were also too set in their ways, colliding with a remarkable new generation of republicans, whose type of lateral thinking was a reaction to their time and circumstance and which confronted the modern British interference in Ireland in every way imaginable.

Comrades of a similar vintage to Ruairí and Dave, republicans like John Joe McGirl, were more broadminded when it came to strategy and recognised the importance of relatively younger leaders, particularly from the North, setting the pace. Conditions under which the struggle were taking place were more intense and complex and unlike anything the Movement had faced in the past.

I was in Dublin by early January 1972.

I went on most of the protests in 1972, including one to the Department of Foreign Affairs. (They allegedly wanted reunification but deal with part of their own country under Foreign Affairs!) This protest, about two weeks before Bloody Sunday, was organised by the Northern Resistance Movement and included among its leaders, Bernadette Devlin and my old friend Michael Farrell. The purpose of the march was 'to break the wall of intolerable complacency and unconcern in the South towards the struggle in the North.'

Then came Bloody Sunday and a huge outburst of anger towards the Brits and sympathy for the North. With the big crowds marching on the British Embassy, and eventually burning it down; with the sympathy there had been for the refugees; for the internees, especially after the reports of men being hooded and tortured, thrown out of helicopters and subjected to mock executions—the government here became extremely alarmed at public opinion swinging towards republicans and the nationalist community. They needed to thwart it, out of self-interest. But rather than confronting the problem, which was British interference in our country, they decided to crush republican resistance to that interference.

The government couldn't wait to effectively support the Brits, the unionists and partition; couldn't wait to kill the aspiration for unity which came with our legitimate demands, whilst posing as critics of British behaviour to satisfy domestic public opinion. It was only the introduction of internment and the anger after Bloody Sunday that forestalled them at the time from introducing Section 31 of the Broadcasting Act to silence the voice of northern nationalists. They got their opportunity after the IRA/British Government truce broke down in July 1972 and with the two car bombs in Dublin in December— planted by loyalists/Brits to influence the outcome of a debate in Leinster House around more repressive legislation, the Offences Against the State Act. Every effort was then made to turn public opinion, to say that republicans were the problem, that the North wasn't that bad, or as bad as the situation had been back when the IRA took up arms against the British during the Tan War.

The refusal of the British to act decisively on rights, their support for the unionists, indulging them, and, indeed, colluding with loyalist paramilitaries in a dirty war of assassination, was meant to sap the will of Irish republicans and defeat out struggle. The British refusal to act, their enthusiasm for repressive laws, and their arming of the loyalists, perpetuated the conflict for decades. We were the ones who wanted peace, real peace, because it was our community that was being militarily occupied and subject to lethal violence and casual brutality.

When I came to live in Dublin in the early Seventies I naturally gravitated to many veteran republicans who had been involved in earlier times. I met Sighle Humphreys first and she introduced me to her fellow 'trouble-maker' Máire Comerford. Sighle was then in her early seventies. My friend, Trisha Ziff, also came with me several times to visit her. Sighle had been a member of Cumann na mBan and was imprisoned in 1922, along with her mother, when the family home was raided by Free State soldiers. During a shoot-out a soldier was killed and Ernie O'Malley, who had been hiding in the house, was seriously wounded. Over the following years Sighle would be jailed seven times—and, as she said herself, ironically, 'Never by the British.' She was also twice on hunger strike, once for thirty-one days. She and Máire had been placed in solitary confinement and Máire was shot and injured by a prison guard. They had also attempted to escape together using an improvised ladder but were caught.

Between Máire, Sighle and myself we shared well over one hundred years of republican activism.

Rita and Máire Comerford

Máire with former Armagh prisoners, Síle Darragh and the late Éilís O'Connor

Máire was living in Sandyford and was still working on her memoirs. She had a vegetable garden behind her cottage in which she still worked, though it was getting hard for her. She had a wee dog that she had found injured outside her house and took him in. She called him Shinner and was heartbroken when he got knocked down and killed. I used to walk from where we were living at the time to visit her. I did not have a car so it was walk or cycle. Máire in her day travelled by pony and trap, by bicycle or walked. So she approved very much of my mode of travel.

Our children loved to visit her with me, to hear her stories of childhood in Wexford where she learned to ride ponies before she could walk. Children were not taught to be afraid in those days, she told them. You learnt to ride and if you fell off you got back on again. You did not, ever, whinge. That spirit she carried with her into her fighting in the Tan War in Cumann na mBan. She was utterly fearless. Her appearance and accent got her out of some dangerous moments as there was an assumption that women of her class could not be involved in this revolution. How wrong they were!

Máire, Sighle and their contemporaries were a formidable force. They fought in the front lines, carried information and communications through enemy lines, often under fire. Máire and Sighle and the majority of the women volunteers rejected the Treaty and fought in, and were imprisoned during, the Civil War. She was in the Four Courts in the thick of the attacks on it. She was in the Hammam Hotel with Cathal Brugha. I can still hear her voice saying these words after Brugha died: 'We were tired, tired, tired and broken-hearted.'

But she and other Cumann na mBan women stood guard at Brugha's coffin. Her heartbreak was for all those who had died in the fight to end British rule and the betrayal of the revolution by the Treaty. The Civil War was even more heartbreak.

Máire talked often and passionately about the need to be vigilant and self-critical, of how essential communications were and how Sinn Féin (this was the 1970s) had to try to overcome the difficulties that Partition posed to an all-Ireland party.

After I was released from Limerick Prison I visited her and found her much frailer. She very much wanted to stay in her own home. Later, when she was wheelchair-bound, my partner Brendan went over and widened the doorframes so she could easily get into her bedroom and bathroom. There were many 'pilgrimages' to her home. I brought former women prisoners down to meet Máire and everybody loved her. My dear friend and comrade Síle Darragh, who had been OC of the women prisoners in Armagh during the 1980 hunger strike, and another former POW, Éilís O'Connor, came to visit after their release.

Danny Morrison would visit with news of the hunger strikes in 1980 and 1981 and stayed overnight a few times. She was not able to visit the H-Blocks but my Brendan and I took her to Portlaoise to visit prisoners there and she was an inveterate writer to republican prisoners. A former prisoner herself, she had great empathy with them. She made all the arrangements for her funeral and wanted Danny Morrison to give her oration. She chose to be buried in Wexford on the side of a mountain where she had run a chicken farm. It was December and it snowed that day.

It was very Máire—no frills, no fuss, but a funeral in a blizzard.

I never realised that my exile would continue for fifty years, so vindictive are the British. My name was raised in the House of Commons despite the later peace process and my political work.

John Taylor had been junior Minister of Home Affairs during the pogroms, the Falls Curfew, the introduction of internment and on Bloody Sunday, and had supported a policy of shoot-to-kill. As a Westminster MP in 1996 he asked for an update on attempts to extradite me. The secretary of state replied, 'The arrest warrant for Ms O'Hare is still outstanding and has not been withdrawn.'

In 1998 Jeffrey Donaldson, now DUP leader, asked another Minister of State what plans there were to arrest me. Adam Ingram replied that although I had escaped (another) extradition attempt in 1978, that 'does not preclude the possibility of the Government seeking Ms O'Hare's extradition if she were to travel to another jurisdiction with which extradition arrangements exist. However, as to the future, it is not the Government's practice to disclose whether or not extradition proceedings are planned.'

In 2022 during a Commons' debate on the Conservative government's planned amnesty for its forces, Ian Paisley Jnr attempted to move an amendment to specifically exclude people like myself. 'If the amendment were to have a name, it would be the "Rita O'Hare amendment",' he said.

Although republicans, including those serving life sentences for major IRA operations in Britain, were released under the Good Friday Agreement, myself and some others were excluded. Owen Carron, Bobby Sands' former election agent, who became an MP after Bobby's death, also faces arrest and prosecution if he crosses the border.

The British continue to retaliate over nationalist demands for truth and the prosecution of state forces involved in collusion and the dirty war and who have enjoyed immunity. In recent years, the British have arrested more republicans than in the early days of the Good Friday Agreement and charged some of them with historic offences. They are sending a warning: 'See what we can do if you continue to demand justice.'

As a result of this, in January 2023, on my eightieth birthday, I'm still 'on the run', so to speak, over a shooting incident in Andersonstown in 1971 when I almost died.

When I moved south I first lived with a family in Dublin, Alice and Des Quinlan. Alice was from a big republican family in Belfast. They were very kind to me. But when my children eventually joined me we went to live in a relatively large house in Goatstown in south Dublin that had been lent to Sinn Féin to temporarily house people from the North and in which there were three other families taking refuge. Ena Browne was living there with her two kids, Julie and Brian, and we loved Ena. Cumann members in Dun Laoghaire arrived with offers of help. People like Mick Egan and Kathleen Knowles. There were always people coming and going and it was there that I got very ill with peritonitis (from one of my wounds) and had to be rushed to St Vincent's Hospital. I knew that Ena would look after my kids. I remember veteran republican John Kelly coming into the hospital and saying, 'You can't go back there. You're too vulnerable.' His wife was a nurse and she was absolutely horrified that somebody who was still convalescing from very, very serious wounds should be living there. When I was moving out some of the other kids wanted to come with me!

My uncle, my mother's youngest brother, was living in Dublin, and he helped get me a house in Monaloe which we lived in for a year or so. Then it was to Granitefield where the rent was much less. The man who owned the house in Granitefield was a decent man. I thought he was very kind. We were there for about five years. I had a terrific neighbour, Eleanor Mooney, who looked out for the kids who got into the local national school and were very settled. Eleanor and I have stayed in contact—she called here last Christmas.

There was very little social welfare in those days for people in my circumstances so just surviving was extremely difficult. I got a job locally with hours that suited, so I was home before the kids got in from school. Rory had access to football which is still his passion. The park was nearby.

The only one that really got restless was Terry. She decided that she wanted to go back to live with Maureen and Billy so she could do the 11-plus exam. I was still thinking in terms of us going back to Belfast, so I reluctantly agreed. She did come back to go to school here later and she still has many friends from back then whom she would visit even now. The kids missed their grandparents, Billy and Maureen, terribly, because they were always a huge part of our lives. And we all missed Margaret Gatt, who had been a wonderful neighbour. I've been very lucky that no matter where we have lived, there has been somebody next door or close by who was a decent, kind person.

My children were nice, they were friendly, so they very quickly made friends despite the Branch knocking on the doors of neighbours, including those whose six-year-old kids were playing with Rory. The neighbours would come and tell me what the Branch had said: 'Do you realise your child is playing with the kids of a terrorist?' To their credit several of those parents told the Branch what they thought of their behavior: 'You're a disgrace. They are children. Leave them alone. I have no problem with my child playing with those children.'

They went to another parent who was a Fianna Fáil councillor. He came and told me. He told the Branch to get away from his door. I always admired him for that. There was another family who made a point of telling their children to play with my kids *because* of what was going on. But an awful lot of people were intimidated. And there might have been some who actually agreed with the Branch. I remember the sense of injustice I felt when I read a letter in one of the newspapers saying something along the lines, 'These people are coming from the North and wanting nice houses with gardens. Who do they think they are?' It bordered on the same racist stereotyping made in recent years by right-wing and fascist groups objecting to immigrants and asylum seekers.

So, the Branch would sit in unmarked vehicles watching the house. They would follow visitors and pull them in and check their ID. Stephen Rea, the actor and a dear friend, was due to visit one day. I'm not sure if he had yet met and married Dolours—she was in jail until 1980. He didn't appear and I thought he had got delayed or waylaid. It turned out that the Branch arrested him coming to my door but I hadn't seen it happen. He was held for several hours.

And there were the occasional house searches. Of course, they were politically directed to do it, though clearly some of them 'enjoyed' their work defending the 'Free State'. With all the revelations that are emerging about the dirty war, the numerous attempts by the British to suppress the truth, to suppress inquests, to legislate amnesty for their intelligence services and their soldiers, in other words to protect themselves, I hope that those people in the South who facilitated the British are deeply ashamed.

Branch car parked outside the Rotunda Hospital. They kept the Sinn Féin offices under constant surveillance from 1970 until 1998

Branchman taking names of those coming out of the Sinn Féin offices in Parnell Square, 1991

In June 1973, while we were still living in Monaloe, a neighbour was going to Dunnes Stores and asked me if I wanted to get my shopping. We set off in her car, the Branch following us. Outside the shop the Branch arrested me. This was on the foot of the first extradition warrant I would face—and fight. I was held in Cabinteely Garda Station. It was filthy. I successfully applied for bail and had to sign on at the Cabinteely Station. One morning when I went to sign on the station was closed. A young Garda appeared but he had no keys. At the back of the station he was able to open a small window but then discovered he was too big to get through. We looked at each other. I said, 'You know, I could get through that but will I be charged with breaking and entering?' I was joking but he responded very seriously and said he didn't think so, 'But please don't tell anybody.' I never did—till now. I climbed in, opened the back door, and we went to the front office where I duly signed the book.

The mood at this time was still one of general sympathy towards the nationalist community. It would not have looked good for the state to hand me over at the border, a young mother of three children still recovering from having been shot by the British Army. As a last resort a defence of political motivation still exempted you from being extradited provided you made a 'statement of claim', which created a Catch 22 situation. In other words, a self-incriminating statement would exempt you before a defence of innocence would. But I didn't need to fall back on that at this stage.

I appeared in court on 4 July, 1973. The kids and some supporters were in the public gallery. I was represented by Ciaran Mac an Aile. Justice Carr asked the inspector if a Ministerial Order had been made as required under Section 28 of the Extradition Act. They hadn't done their homework and the inspector tried to buy time. The judge, in one of those rare acts of judicial independence, which would wane over the years as the government streamlined the law in submission to Britain, said: 'This Court is not a rubber stamp for the State or any agency of the State.'

He dismissed the warrant and I was free to go.

Although the power-sharing agreement collapsed in May 1974 the only part of the Sunningdale Agreement that survived was the Criminal Law Jurisdiction Act which was aimed at making extradition easier.

CHAPTER SIX

BACK TO PRISON

It was February 1975 and I was visiting Portlaoise Prison. Peter Lynch was a republican prisoner from County Derry. There were other prisoners and visitors in the room. After our visit he was stopped and searched and was found in possession of four ounces of plastic explosives concealed in a condom. Later that night our house was raided and I was arrested and brought to the Bridewell, questioned about visiting the prison. I denied smuggling the explosives into the jail.

I'm not going to go into the exact details of what happened but it is something I deeply regret. It was done and that's it. I was solely responsible—and I was totally irresponsible—and it had a profound, traumatic effect on the lives and wellbeing of my kids. I still carry the guilt. Of all the things I have done it is one of the things that I deeply regret.

I was charged and appeared in court. My solicitor was Myles Shevlin and I had a great barrister, Patrick McEntee, who succeeded in getting me bail. It was £10,000 in total and I had to report daily to Cabinteely Garda Station between 9 am and 9 pm.

Three prison officers gave evidence at the non-jury trial two months later. One said it was possible that another visitor might have handed over the explosives while two said they saw me pass a small item. I contested the charges. But I was sentenced to three years' penal servitude despite Peter trying to get me off by making an unsworn statement that I was not involved. He received a sentence of six years on top of the five he was already serving.

We had just managed to be settled in a house and now the lives of Terry, Frances and Rory were once again turned upside down. Billy and Maureen were wonderful.

Gerry O'Hare had been arrested in 1973 when the Gardaí raided a press conference at the launch of the pamphlet, *Freedom Struggle*, and he was sentenced on a charge of IRA membership. While in prison he had received another sentence for helping in the helicopter escape from Mountjoy Jail but he was out by this time, and though we were separated, he agreed to look after the children. But some of the time they were in Belfast, some in Dublin, and their schooling suffered major disruption. He was also in another relationship. The kids, by and large, don't hold this against me, and I love and admire them for all that they experienced and survived, but I haven't, nor will I ever get over it.

Back then divorce was illegal in the South and it would be almost another twenty-five years before it became law. Gerry and I eventually divorced in the early 1990s.

Just before my arrest in relation to Portlaoise I had met and struck up a relationship with a Belfast republican, Brendan Brownlee, whom I had met briefly when I was in Belfast.

The conflict broke many families, broke many family bonds. It was mostly men—often referred to as 'the bread winners'—who went to prison, not mothers. I relied on many friends to take care of my kids and one such friend was Kathleen Knowles and her partner Dermot McGurk.

My kids were particularly vulnerable because unlike the bonds and supports that exist in West Belfast they weren't in a neighbourhood where families were in the same position or among a community with an understanding of why somebody would take the risk that I did. I would, supposedly, have only be gone for a few hours on a prison visit to Portlaoise then I'd be back home afterwards. Instead, there they were, the only kids whose mother was in jail for anything. That was very difficult for them. I could understand people being really disapproving that I would risk that. I disapprove of myself for having risked that when I had small children. The school was pretty good—reasonably supportive. And they had settled in so well.

So, I was taken to Limerick Prison.

On my first visit the prison officers brought me into a room in a stone building, not where the usual visits took place. In the room they had built a wooden box with a window in it. They wanted me to go in and look at the kids through a window. I refused. Terry tried to run over to me and was roughly dragged out. Gerry rightly took them out and said this is utterly unacceptable, that we could barely see each other or talk to each other. The kids were all really upset about that and certainly didn't want to come back where they couldn't even touch me or barely hear me. None of the other republican women would take visits.

Gardaí gather outside Limerick Prison before protestors arrive to demonstrate against family visiting restrictions. Courtesy: *Limerick Leader*

Prison life was not unduly harsh in comparison to life for a republican in an English prison or what the women in Armagh would shortly be subjected to. My concern wasn't whether today's meal would be lukewarm or cold or unappetising. I couldn't have cared less. My thoughts were outside with Terry, Rory and Frances and whether they were being properly cared for, because by now my marriage had been effectively over for some time.

Limerick was different from my two experiences of Armagh, particularly my second imprisonment after the introduction of internment when the administration began to realise it was going to be confronting a lot of determined republican women. I've already mentioned how many of the screws in Armagh were born-again Christians, out to save our souls from hellfire and damnation. In the North, political imprisonment was part of the nationalist culture and experience and we were regularly kept informed about political developments and local news. Even after the visits protest in Limerick was resolved, there were so few of us, and fewer visits, we were fairly cut off. The regime also wanted to avoid any trouble. But we had each other for support. I was able to concentrate on reading and I remember the doctor expressing surprise at seeing books on anti-colonialism and books by Albert Camus and Sartre on my shelf, as if we were supposed to be illiterate.

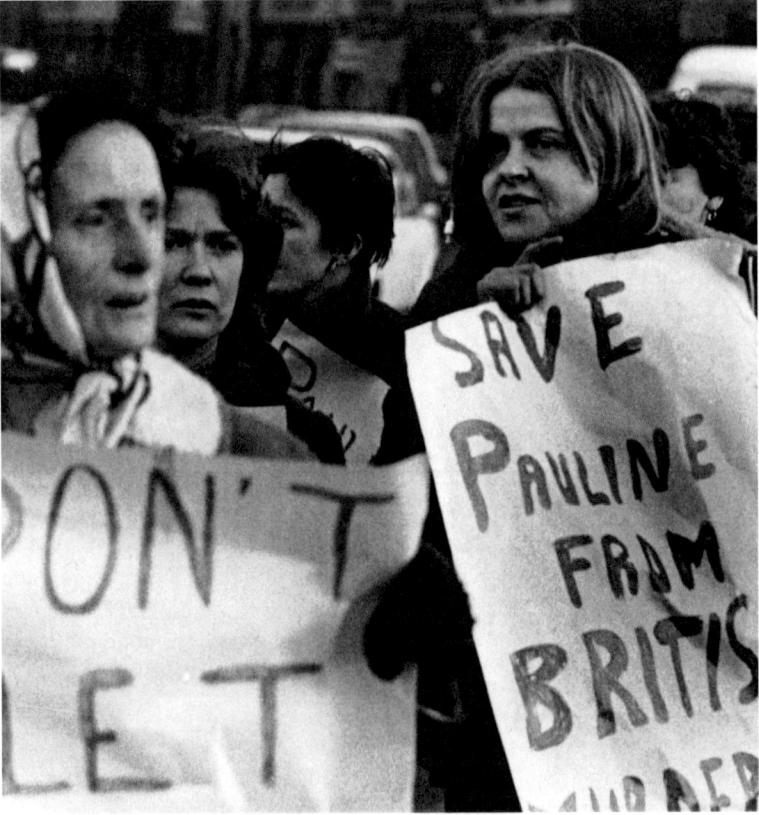

Rita and Rose at a prison protest after their release

There was a recreation room with a television where we could watch the news but we were not allowed personal radios. There were communal loudspeakers in each cell but the master radio was only tuned to one station.

It was in Limerick that I first met Rose Dugdale when there was a knock on my cell door shortly after I arrived. I looked through the spyhole to see Rose with this most beautiful baby in her arms. Ruairi was a few months old and had been born in the prison. She had been pregnant when she was arrested. She was sentenced to nine years.

The regime was so obsessed that she might escape that they had brought a doctor and midwife into the jail rather than allow her to give birth in an outside hospital under guard, as was the normal practice. (We used to quite deliberately pretend to be hatching escape plans—it was just entertainment for us, to wind the staff up.)

59

The prison regime could be punitive in very petty ways in the restriction of letters and withholding books or clothes sent in from family or friends. Rose discovered that a lot of people had sent baby clothes to her for Ruairi. She was only given them when she was released. I was given a lot of letters, including from my children that had been withheld, and I am sure the others had the same experience.

Rose was delighted that in me she had someone who knew something about kids. We got on terrifically. She is a very kind person. But what the papers said about her, how the media tried to demonise her as an eccentric adventurer was a disgrace, was absolute nonsense. Yes, she had been born into wealth and privilege in England but she wasn't a crazy person—not at all. She made a considered choice. She had been in other movements in England, fighting against class inequality. When she found out about Ireland she decided to devote herself to supporting the cause of freedom. She wasn't the only English or American or other nationality that saw the injustice and decided to do something about it. True, they were few in number but she was not unique. Of course there was some things she didn't fully understand about Ireland but she was certainly willing to listen and learn. Rose loved practical jokes, which sometimes were not appreciated by the recipients. One favourite was balancing buckets of dirty water on the top of doors for the unwary.

In 1975, Marion Coyle from Derry was jailed. She and Eddie Gallagher, Ruairi's father, had kidnapped an industrialist and demanded the release of Rose and two others, but were arrested after the negotiated end to a siege of a house in Monasterevin where they had been holding the businessman, Tiede Herrema.

Rose's family came to visit her but it wouldn't have been very often because they were elderly and had to travel a great distance.

Marion came from a large family but her visitors had a long journey from Derry to visit Limerick, about a twelve-hour round trip back then when there were no dual carriageways.

I—and Rose—got a real sense of the appalling poverty in the South— the extremely hard lives of some of the other prisoners. Women who had been driven to prostitution out of poverty. A Traveller who was imprisoned for stealing a bar of soap. Young Traveller women who couldn't read or write. But that was common: they weren't the only ones. There was no literacy programme offered to them. Most of these women were serving short sentences. They were simply put in a cell for three or six months and then let go. There was no support given, no questions asked about whether they had somewhere to live upon release. As I mentioned, when I first came to live here in the early 1970s there was little or no right to social welfare. There was nothing. It was like the deserving poor and you had to go and beg for it. The changes since, the rights that had to be fought for, and which were won, are many, but there remain many, many battles ahead, also to be won.

Another prisoner was Marie Murray who along with her husband Noel had been sentenced to death. They had been anarchists and were convicted for the killing of an off-duty Garda officer, Michael Reynolds, following a Dublin bank robbery in 1975. She took her death sentence so calmly it was remarkable. After a big campaign they were retried and their sentence was commuted to life imprisonment. Marie was a *gaeilgeoir* and with her I tried to brush up my Irish. She was a lovely woman, a very quiet person.

Angela Duffin of the INLA was also in with us. She was from Belfast and so we had that connection. And that was about it for *politicals*.

We were always looking for ways to pass the time though of course we talked a lot about political issues. We read as many books as we could get.

The odd time there was a couple of ordinary prisoners. But it was a very small number: the women's wing in Limerick was tiny. One prisoner, I think her name was Margaret, was a really good knitter and offered to teach us. I thought it could be a way to show the children how much we missed them and thought about them. There was some difficulty at first getting the governor to agree to us getting knitting needles but we prevailed. Margaret also showed us how to crochet and Rose was very good at it. I stuck to the knitting and loved being able to send out winter jumpers to my kids. Angela proved to be the best as she could sew and the screws let her use a sewing machine that was in the recreation room. She taught herself to use it and could cut patterns and made some beautiful clothes for her wee niece.

Marian did a lot of art work, she had a natural talent for drawing and design. I know this does not sound like the mad revolutionaries we were portrayed as but it passed the time and the kids loved the results of our endeavours.

Some news of our protest against the visiting restrictions, which went on for months, made it into the papers but not much.

As for the Women's Movement back then, few feminists took up the issue of these unacceptable visiting conditions for families. They would have been more concerned about women in jails anywhere in the world except Ireland; seemed to me more concerned about women priests and women being allowed into golf clubs. Sadly, you see this in many radical groups whose priorities are tailored to safe and virtuous causes.

Many years later, in the mid-Eighties, I was a speaker at an Irish National Women's Conference in Dublin. There were delegates from EI Salvador, South Africa and the Six Counties who all participated in a session on 'National Struggle'. The conference applauded the Salvadoran and Southern African women—who were saying basically the same things as the republican women—but condemned women in the antiimperialist struggle against the British.

Too close to home, you see.

However, there were exceptions—really good women, such as Nell McCafferty from Derry and Sylvia Meehan from Dublin. For Nell it was not just a feminist issue but related to her entire experience as an excluded northern nationalist, to her experiences of the injustice of partition. She would later write an important book, *The Armagh Women*, highlighting conditions there and the 1980 hunger strike of Mairéad Farrell, Mary Doyle and Mairéad Nugent. I can still recall the startling first line of an article she wrote in the *Irish Times* in 1981: 'There is menstrual blood on the walls of Armagh prison in Northern Ireland', which shockingly challenged feminists. The late Sylvia Meehan was a feminist and trade unionist who, like Nell, wasn't intimidated by the establishment, the media, or the 'delicacy' of her colleagues—and spoke out against injustice. She opposed the non-jury Special Criminal Court and spoke out about the torture of those falsely accused of the Sallins Train Robbery, who were mostly members of the Irish Republican Socialist Party.

I was due to be released on 14 April but I knew something was wrong when on the 13 April the cells were not opened after lunch and screws came to my door and told me to get my stuff together. I asked what was happening but they refused to tell me. I suspected there was another attempt afoot to serve me with an extradition order, my second. They could have served this at any time over the past few years but waited until the end of my sentence. I was able to say a quick goodbye to the other prisoners before being hustled down the stairs and out into a waiting car. Because this was sprung on me I'd no way of notifying my solicitor. I was driven to Mountjoy Prison and put in a cell overnight. The only other female political prisoner there at the time was Chrissie McAuley from Belfast who was serving four years.

Next morning, just after 8 am I was taken to an exit door but was immediately rearrested and served by Detective Sergeant Patrick Morgan with an extradition warrant to have me sent North. It alleged that on 25 October 1971 in Andersonstown I and another person unknown shot Warrant Officer Fraser Paton with intent to kill him. I made no reply.

From Mountjoy I was taken to the Dublin District Court and appeared before Judge Donal Kearney. The state solicitor Robert Barr opposed my bail application but my solicitor Greg Murphy said I had honoured my previous bail commitments. Kearney, after considering the issue, granted me bail of £500. I could see my family in the court. We met in an office while bail was being organised and for the first time in two years I was able to hug Rory and Frances, my children.

The excitement at getting home and seeing the children was dimmed by finding out that there was an eviction order on the house. The rent had not been paid in months. I had no knowledge of this and no warning that my urgent task now was to find somewhere in the area at an affordable rent. Furthermore, I'd a pony in the garden, without fodder or a stable. Gerry had left it as a present for Frances.

Terry, Frances and Rory were all at school in the area and doing well. They never had problems with school work, so I wanted to find somewhere that would not necessitate them changing schools. Life had not been easy for them, particularly while I was away. They had friends in Granitefield and I had some good neighbours who looked out for them as much as they could. But I was gutted when they told me that the only time they really felt safe and secure during those two years was when they were with their grandparents Maureen and Billy, particularly during holidays.

The landlord in Granitefield gave me time to try to find somewhere. But it was impossible. I simply could not afford the rent of any house in the area.

Brendan was living with friends Mick and Linda Egan. We talked over the situation. He was very positive, very supportive and wanted us to live together. He got on really well with Terry, Frances and Rory. He moved in—not with four people, but *five*, and a pony in the garden! Before learning about the eviction notice I had promised a friend, who was pregnant and due to give birth in May, that I would foster her baby until she got settled in a new home. Brendan and I went together to meet the new addition, Ciaran, who was just six days old. We all fell in love with him, and with his mother's agreement Brendan and I later joyfully adopted Ciaran. He brought so many wonderful moments to our life.

We discussed what to do—whether to pay a big rent or try for council housing. I was eventually offered a flat in Ballinteer. Again it was members of the local Sinn Féin Cumann who offered help. Two of them wallpapered and painted it as it was in poor condition and filthy, and others, including Des Quinlan and Deasún Breatnach, helped us to move.

Brendan was a hard worker, had some men working for him, and he worked at restoring some of the beautiful old Georgian houses in Dublin. We saved as much as we could. Back then it was relatively easy to get a mortgage.

In July 1977 I was again ordered to be handed over to the RUC at the border but various legal proceedings halted that although I, Brendan and the children lived everyday under fear of that threat. It came to court in March 1978 and again I was represented by Greg Murphy, Ciaran Mac an Aile and Patrick McEntee. I signed an affidavit which was read to Justice D'Arcy. My arrest and being charged in 1971 preceded the retrogressive changes to extradition law and I could still claim exemption by stating that my actions fell into the category of 'a political offence or an offence connected to a political offence.' The affidavit stated that I had joined the IRA and had taken part in an ambush of British soldiers in Andersonstown. D'Arcy then halted my extradition.

And those were my circumstances when the manager Mick Timothy asked me to join the staff of *An Phoblacht*. I found a childminder for Ciaran and began working in 44 Parnell Square.

Ciaran on the day of his First Holy Communion

CHAPTER SEVEN

1981 – THE HUNGER STRIKES

While writing for *An Phoblacht* presented a fresh, new challenge, I felt fairly confident. I wrote all my articles in longhand—and they were legible! Although it had been many years since I had written a school essay, I had read widely in literature, philosophy and politics and had been involved in political debate for a dozen years. There was a library in Limerick, for the male prisoners. We got books in now and again. I read most of the Russian classics and French writers like Sartre. And, of course, my Da, Billy, had already inculcated into me an appreciation of ideology! But when supplies were lean there were times, I have to confess, when I resorted to reading cowboy books!

When I was released in April 1977 the blanket protest in the H-Blocks was about eight months old, started by Kieran Nugent from Belfast who over the next few years would be joined by hundreds of others, mostly very young people. They were working class or from poor rural areas, from communities which had suffered deprivation and discrimination for decades. Kieran, who was serving a relatively short sentence of three years, lost in total 519 days remission for refusing to wear the prison uniform and call the prison officers, 'Sir'. Almost all of the prison officers were from a unionist background and a large number of them were former British soldiers who had served in the North and married local women.

The rejection of the authority and legitimacy of their jailers is well-recognised in republican penal history, so when Britain took the decision to 'criminalise' the republican struggle they were well aware of the past history of resistance, including the tradition of hunger striking against injustice. Nevertheless, they set out with the objective of 'criminalising' the prisoners as part of a crusade to 'criminalise' and demoralise the struggle for Irish independence. It was part of their war of attrition. And the prisoners—although outwardly the argument was around conditions and formal recognition of their political status—understood exactly the implications and the wider stakes.

Successive Irish governments also knew that a victory for the prisoners would be a victory in the struggle to end partition. The establishment had become comfortable and used to operating within the Twenty-Six Counties. The hostility to northern republicans and defiant nationalists from leadership figures in Fine Gael and Fianna Fáil, the Special Branch, and mainstream media columnists and RTÉ presenters was unbridled, cowardly and shameful, acting out of self-interest, but also subconscious self-loathing.

The responsibility for bringing about the resulting chaos and suffering associated with the prison crisis was the British Government's. In 1972 the British had 'settled' the prison issue by recognising that the conflict was political in nature and that those convicted as a result of it would be treated in a separate, 'special category'—that is they would have political status. Thus, sentenced prisoners were housed in Nissen huts, three huts to each cage in Long Kesh Prison Camp, but separated from the internees' cages. (The authorities referred to the living quarters as 'compounds' rather than cages.)

In 1976, the British reneged on this earlier agreement and sought to criminalise the prisoners and the republican cause. They had many allies. They divided the site at Long Kesh. They'd already changed its name to The Maze in an attempt to escape the international opprobrium associated with the POW camp and their maltreatment of prisoners. The media and politicians dutifully echoed the new name—as if Long Kesh had closed down. In one part of this vast prison were the Cages in which internees, and sentenced prisoners with political status, were held. In the other half they built the H-Blocks. However, according to a Northern Ireland Office planning paper, the British were aware from the outset that 'any prison at the Maze site will never be able to disassociate itself from Long Kesh political prison image.'

From the propaganda and rhetoric of politicians and the media, especially in the South, you would never have known that the British created the prison crisis. Their default position was that republicans were to blame for the violence and thus they were ultimately to blame for everything that subsequently occurred. These critics might also meekly suggest some minor changes to prison rules—but never for the return of full political status or the implementation of the 'five demands' as formulated by the Relatives Action Committees and the National Smash H-Block/Armagh Committee.

These campaigning groups did brilliant work, raising the issue, organising marches and lobbying. Almost every picket, every demonstration, every march was harassed by the RUC, the UDR and the British Army. People were stopped, their IDs checked on their way to a march and when leaving a march. Cars were stopped, buses were stopped and delayed. Soldiers would go through the instruments of bands, search everyone, all with the objective of interrupting peaceful protest. Activists were targeted by loyalist paramilitaries—who were really proxy state forces—and several were shot dead, including university lecturer Miriam Daly and Irish Independence Party Councillor John Turnly. Bernadette Devlin (McAliskey) and her husband Michael were also shot and seriously injured in their home, while British soldiers observed from a distance.

Others who raised their heads above the parapet was the lawyer and founder of People's Democracy, Michael Farrell; the editor of the *Irish Press*, Tim Pat Coogan, who visited Armagh and the H-Blocks and wrote the book *On The Blanket*; Mary Holland (who was sacked from *The Observer* for writing about the mother of a blanket man); Christy Moore, Donal Lunny and their band Moving Hearts, and the Wolfe Tones. Bobby Ballagh the artist and Stephen Rea the actor, and several brave priests all spoke out, while others, the majority, shamefully buried their heads in the sand and ignored the brutality, just up the road, 'Ninety miles from Dublin town,' as Christy Moore put it in his song. Their pretext for remaining silent was that to speak out would only encourage support for the IRA—when the truth was that their silence only encouraged state violence and gave the British succour that they could do whatever they liked.

There is no doubt that the deliberate attempts to ignore the prison protest prolonged the protest and the suffering, and prolonged a resolution being reached. But it also backfired on the British and Dublin governments. Within the Catholic hierarchy there were those like Bishop Cahal Daly who discouraged the British Government from engaging with the republican leadership over *anything*. In contrast, there were a small number of clerics such as Fr Joe McVeigh, Fr Des Wilson, Fr Alec Reid, Fr Brian Brady, and prison chaplains Fr Raymond Murray and Fr Denis Faul, who spoke out. Archbishop Ó Fiaich (later, Cardinal) made a powerful statement after visiting the H-Blocks about six-months into the no-wash protest. In any similar situation you would expect such an intervention on a human rights' issue would discomfort the establishment and result in some curtailment of abuse, or would become a benchmark for politicians, journalists and commentators in assessing rights and wrongs. Not so when it came to Ó Fiaich speaking in August 1978. I remember the buzz around 44 (our office) after Ó Fiaich's remarks and the initial publicity his visit to the jail engendered. He said:

'I was shocked at the inhuman conditions prevailing in H-Blocks Three, Four and Five, where over 300 prisoners were incarcerated. One would hardly allow an animal to remain in such conditions, let alone a human being. The nearest approach to it that I have seen was the spectacle of hundreds of homeless people living in the sewer pipes in the slums of Calcutta. The stench and filth in some of the cells, with the remains of rotten food and human excreta scattered around the walls was almost unbearable. In two of them I was unable to speak for fear of vomiting.

'The prisoners' cells are without beds, chairs or tables. They sleep on mattresses on the floor and, in some cases, I noticed that these were quite wet. They have no covering except a towel or blanket, no books, newspapers or reading material except the Bible (even religious magazines have been banned since my last visit), no pens or writing materials, no TV or radio, no hobbies or handicrafts, no exercise or recreation. They are locked in their cells for almost the whole of every day, and some of them have been in this condition for more than a year and a half …

'It is evident that they intend to continue their protest indefinitely and it seems they prefer to face death rather than to submit to being classed as criminals. Anyone with the least knowledge of Irish history knows how deeply this attitude is in our country's past. In isolation and perpetual boredom, they maintain their sanity by studying Irish. It was an indication of the triumph of the human spirit over adverse material conditions to notice Irish words, phrases and songs being shouted from cell to cell and then written on each cell wall with the remnants of toothpaste tubes.'

The Northern Ireland Office expressed surprise at Archbishop Ó Fiaich's statement and reiterated the British Government's determination to 'stand firm in its policy' on criminalisation. Earlier, British Labour Junior Minister Don Concannon, a horrible person, said, 'There are going to be no concessions on the question of special treatment for prisoners, no matter how such treatment may be described.'

Ó Fiaich had also criticised the authorities for their refusal 'to admit that these prisoners are in a different category from the ordinary, yet everything about their trials and family background indicates that they are different. They were sentenced by special courts without juries … The vast majority were convicted on allegedly voluntary confessions obtained in circumstances which are now placed under grave suspicion by the recent report of Amnesty International. Many are very youthful and come from families which had never been in trouble with the law, though they lived in areas which suffered discrimination in housing and jobs. How can one explain the jump in the prison population of Northern Ireland from 500 to 3,000 unless a new type of prisoner has emerged?

'The problem of these prisoners is one of the great obstacles to peace in our community. As long as it continues it will be a potent cause of resentment in the prisoners themselves, breeding frustration among their relatives and friends and leading to bitterness between the prisoners and the prison staff. It is only sowing the seeds of future conflict.'

When I began writing for *An Phoblacht*, our other paper, *Republican News,* was still being produced in the North under Danny Morrison, though its staff had endured gun and bomb attacks and its offices had been regularly raided and editions of the paper seized at the printers. *An Phoblacht* had also suffered regular raids and Gardaí harassment. Several editors of the paper were arrested and charged with IRA membership under the Offences Against the State Act. In the case of Éamonn Mac Thomáis he was sentenced to fifteen months. Upon release he returned to the paper only to be arrested weeks later, charged again and sentenced to another fifteen months. Tim Pat Coogan, then editor of the *Irish Press,* condemned the charges as politically motivated as Éamonn's activities were confined strictly to republican journalism. Éamonn, who as a historian had also produced documentaries for RTÉ, was banned from the airwaves.

This was how vindictive the establishment in the South was.

In April 1978 the Brits made the biggest attempt yet to close down *Republican News.* Most of its staff were arrested and charged and imprisoned in Armagh Jail and Crumlin Road, including the printer in Lurgan, businessman Gary Kennedy, a member of the SDLP who was charged with IRA membership, a preposterous allegation but one aimed at intimidating all other northern printers.

At *An Phoblacht* Deasún Breatnach was the editor and Mick Timothy the business manager. In January 1975, Mick had left

Working in *An Phoblacht/Republican News*

Manchester to escape imminent arrest for his republican activities and came to live in Dublin. He was billeted with a well-known republican family, the Sillerys of Drimnagh, and in true romantic tradition fell in love and married a daughter of the house, Alice, in August 1975.

In late January 1979 our two newspapers merged as *An Phoblacht/Republican News* with Danny as editor and Mick as manager. But Mick now began to write—and it turned out he was brilliant. Sharp, witty, droll, dedicated. When Danny was elected to the Northern assembly in 1982 he stood down and Mick became editor. He wrote an eagerly-awaited weekly column, 'Burke's at the Back', in which he tore shreds off the parties here, their hypocrisy and double standards. His 1984 feature, *Béal na mBláther*, was a *tour de force* for its attack on revisionism and how Fine Gael and Fianna Fáil glorified 'the good old IRA' while condemning those fighting in worse conditions in the North for the same aspiration of Irish independence and an end to British rule. Their utter hypocrisy was not lost on people.

He made several innovative changes in the paper, not least the major expansion from twelve to sixteen pages. This allowed for a greater coverage of social, economic and political issues throughout the thirty-two counties as well as introducing a lighter side to the paper with review pages and of course his own extremely popular column. It often made some people see red, the same colour as *AP/RN*'s masthead. Mick changed the masthead from green to red, which generated a great deal of controversy both in our letters page and at two Ard Fheiseanna. One of the reasons it stayed red, as he explained at the 1983 Ard Fheis, was because Mick liked the colour red!

71

Mick encouraged controversy in the columns of the paper. It made *AP/RN* interesting and reflected the views of the readership. Another new departure for the paper, encouraged by Mick, was the use of full-colour photographs on our front page which first appeared just after his death. He always strove to make *AP/RN* relevant, accurate and professional. Mick's standards were high: standards that were a result of his commitment to the Republican Movement as well as his obvious ability.

He held several prominent roles in Sinn Féin and was on the Ard Chomhairle. He sat on the planning and research committees. He was head of the strategy committee for the EEC elections in 1984, where his ability to analyse political situations and pinpoint areas for action ensured that Sinn Féin always had a position on whatever were the issues of the day. On top of all this he was in his last year of studying law at the Kings Inns in Dublin, and achieved the distinction of being one of the best of his year. He was devoted to his wife Alice and to their children, Ciara, Fiachra and Fionan. Despite the great pressures on him from both his republican activities and his law studies, he never failed to be a conscientious and loving husband and father who spent as much time as he could with his family.

His premature death in 1985 robbed the struggle of a brilliant intellect and critical voice. He had no time for humbug or opportunism. Another, later editor, Mícheál Mac Donncha, wrote a tribute to Mick, detailing his life in Manchester which is where he joined the Republican Movement in the early 1970s and was active in Sinn Féin. He recalled an incident from the early 1970s when Mick organised the Manchester Martyrs Commemoration—before escaping to Dublin to avoid arrest. He was drilling the republican colour party in a public park. Commands were being issued in Irish and the ranks were marching up and down military-style, when a passer-by alerted the Manchester police. A patrol arrived to investigate.

'What's going on?' asked a policeman. Mick responded, in his heavy Manchester accent, that they were a band. 'Where's your instruments, then?' asked the policeman, to which Mick replied: 'We're a marching band—we're practising marching first.'

Typical Mick.

Our typesetters in the newly-merged paper were my old friend Kathleen Knowles, Mick's wife Alice; and Eileen Magee from Belfast, who was married to Pat Magee, later sentenced for the Brighton Bombing. Eileen lived with her young son in Ballymun flats. Danny Devenny, a former political prisoner and artist (and later, muralist) from Belfast, designed the paper, and Phil Shemeld, formerly of the Troops Out Movement, was a sub-editor. Typesetters also came down every week and worked uncomplainingly in the office for many, many long hours over two or three intense days. There was Jackie Burt, who had worked for the Green Cross in West Belfast. Also from Belfast came Chrissie McAuley (at the time, pregnant, and who had served time in Mountjoy Jail) and Mary Hickey who were both in 44 the night a loyalist gunman opened fire and wounded Danny and another member of our staff, Pat Magee. Incredibly, Danny came back from the hospital to finish the paper.

People worked on the paper for literally 'buttons', yet North and South we continued to attract talented young people who sacrificed more lucrative opportunities in life and careers for a commitment that was not easy and involved enduring harassment, threats and abuse and even physical attack. It is truly remarkable when you think back on it. It is probably why we are where we are today.

A few months after I became editor in 1985 young Mark Dawson from Dublin joined the paper as a graphic designer and he is still with the publicity department to this day, almost forty years later. He is a great archivist and can put his hand on any article or feature you need from any of those years. He helped me enormously when I went to work in the USA. Danny Morrison had devised a series of pop-up banners about the history of hunger striking, Irish republicanism and British colonialism, which made for a brilliant exhibition. Mark was able to make perfect scans of the high resolution graphics and sent them to me electronically which we then printed in the States. It went all around the States.

We were publishing book reviews, film reviews, war news from the North; news of the anti-apartheid campaign regarding South Africa; Angola, Mozambique and East Timor, after the withdrawal of the Portuguese colonial army; Palestine, Central and South America. The camaraderie was extraordinary. We were all part of a living national and international struggle. Gestures of solidarity can be seen almost weekly in our journalism in *An Phoblacht/Republican News,* and in the speakers who were given a platform at Ard Fheiseanna. We debated feminism, capitalism, gay rights, divorce, the environment, in our periodicals and at conference.

We had great writers like Brian McDonald and John Hedges. Brian will never forget to tell you that he is from Clones! In August 1981, upon returning to his London flat from a visit to Belfast, John was arrested by the Special Branch and held in Paddington

Green for three days. After his release he immediately flew to Dublin with nothing but a holdall with some clothes. All his republican friends were in Belfast and he knew no one here. Brendan and I saw him at a commemoration in Dún Laoghaire and we could see he was trying to find his bearings. We took him under our wing and invited him back to our house. The kids engaged in some innocent banter about his English accent. He became a regular visitor thereafter and we remain great friends after forty years. John was the best copywriter and proof-reader ever.

Unfortunately, I cannot remember everyone that contributed back then, so my apologies. But we had reporters all around the country feeding us local news about the hunger-strike campaign which was extensive. Many protests and marches were ignored by their local media or if covered never made it into the national press.

The focus of much of our coverage in this period was on the prison protests and solidarity activities. We'd publish prison comms (smuggled letters) and poetry and short stories under the name Marcella—who was actually Bobby Sands. In our northern office in Belfast Richard and Chrissie McAuley and Jim Gibney were our main journalists. They would interview family members or recently-released prisoners who would describe conditions and beatings. Chrissie was particularly good in drawing out from interviewees descriptions and emotions, the atmosphere during destructive house raids, furniture broken, a newly-decorated bedroom destroyed, tearing open of kids' Christmas presents … that sort of thing.

But it was impossible to escape thoughts about what was going on in the prisons. I used to think: how can the prisoners endure what is being done to them?

I am proud of the work we did—we created a record in minor and great detail. But you also had this nagging feeling—could you have done more? Writing is so important: to put down on paper, for the record, the experiences of ordinary people, especially the oppressed, for their stories to enter history. Governments hate being challenged which is why they use censorship, censure good journalists, and pour their vast resources into propaganda, official notices and advertisements.

In October 1980 seven blanket men went on hunger strike, led by Brendan Hughes. Bobby Sands took over as OC of the Blocks. Three women joined the strike on 1 December, led by Mairéad Farrell whose position as OC was then taken over by Síle Darragh. The other two were

Mary Doyle and Mairéad Nugent. This was Mary's second time in jail. She had already served a five-year sentence and had political status. Whilst in prison her mother, Marie, was killed by a loyalist no-warning bomb. The women's hunger strike was overshadowed by the men in the H-Blocks, for a variety of reasons. Of course, there were more reports from the Blocks because there were hundreds of men on the blanket suffering regular beatings. Unlike in the Blocks the women were no longer forced to wear the despised prison uniform but still they suffered terrible deprivations for refusing to do punitive work. They were denied routine exercise in fresh air, available to conforming prisoners; denied association with each other; denied routine visits with family; denied food parcels to supplement the diet of often inedible prison food; denied newspapers, magazines, books and writing material. They had been denied access to the toilets and had been assaulted by male prison officers specially drafted into the women's prison and were, like the blanket men, on the no wash protest.

While the blanket protest was ignored for years, the women's protest was covered even less. The lack of coverage might also be attributed to prevailing misogyny which was so much a part of male-dominated society.

I felt guilty that we should have done more on Armagh—though what we could have done better confounds me. The women were much smaller in number than the men and were more isolated and this took its toll, physiologically and psychologically. The screws continually tried to demoralise them, often goading them with, 'You're on your own! Nobody cares! It's your own fault!' They were incredibly strong, dedicated young women and sacrificed so much—especially because they were incarcerated during their child-bearing years.

Late into the hunger strike the British were in contact with the republican leadership through what's been called the 'back channel'— which was a totally unsatisfactory form of communication because messages were going through an intermediary (who could distort or finesse what either side were saying and you wouldn't know). Also, the British insisted on 'deniability' should the back channel become public. Still, it was republican lives which were at stake and any opportunity to save lives had to be grasped. Understandably, there was huge distrust and suspicion.

On 18 December a British representative flew to Aldergrove Airport and handed over a document about prison reform to Fr Brendan Meagher, a Redemptorist priest. Before this document was delivered to

Michael Gaughan

Frank Stagg

Bobby Sands

Francis Hughes

Raymond McCreesh

Patsy O'Hara

the strikers in the prison hospital Brendan Hughes called off the hunger strike which was into its fifty-third day.

The women heard the news on a smuggled radio but were skeptical and when the governor told Mairéad Farrell that the hunger strike in the Blocks was over she refused to accept his word, fearing he was playing psychological games. Later, that night Danny Morrison went to Armagh Prison but was refused a visit with Mairéad. Only the next day, when Fr Meagher confirmed the news did the women end their strike.

Joe McDonnell

Martin Hurson

Kevin Lynch

Kieran Doherty

Thomas McElwee

Mickey Devine

With the hunger strike having ended just before the arrival of the British document, the Brits and the prison administration then felt there was no need to proceed with implementing progressive reforms that would resolve the political status issue. This intransigence, and the triumphalist attitude of prison staff, triggered the much bigger and more profound second hunger strike in 1981 which would see the deaths of ten blanket men. Also—and this is something we should never forget—all those senior politicians and clerics who had called upon the prisoners to end the hunger strike, with the guarantee that in a less-confrontational atmosphere they could and would then exert pressure on the Brits: well, they disappeared once they thought the prisoners had been defeated.

There was a lesson in this: we republicans must always, first and foremost, rely on ourselves, on our own strength, determination and will. Without republicans driving the agenda—socially, economically, politically, around the lives of those struggling in their identity and for human respect, around reunification—there will be no change in this country.

The Officer Commanding the women in Armagh during the 1980 hunger strike was Síle Darragh from Ballymacarrett in east Belfast—coincidentally a short distance from where my Da, Billy, was born in 1911 in Rosebery Road. It was after her release that we became best friends. Síle is very self-effacing and private, but somehow she was persuaded—a bit like myself—to write about her experiences in Armagh Prison. Her book, with the wry title, *John Lennon's Dead*, is a wonderful and honest account of a young female leader dealing with the awesome nature of British power over her and her comrades' lives.

An Phoblacht/Republican News came out on a Thursday and on Fridays the editorial staff would meet at 44, review that week's issue and plan for the following week. The prison crisis dominated those meetings. All of us used whatever contacts we had to muster statements of support for the five demands. It was the same on the ard comhairle: the prison issue and hunger strike dominated business for months, if not years on end.

When news came of a second hunger strike to be led by Bobby Sands, I remember the journalist Mary Holland asking me whether I thought the British Government would let Bobby die.

'Let him die? Yes, they will. And more than Bobby.'

In 1974 and 1976 two IRA prisoners, Michael Gaughan and Frank Stagg, suffered horrific deaths on hunger strike in English prisons against an almost-total media blackout.

Mary was a highly respected journalist and had written extensively on the North, at times terrifically. She was sacked from *The Observer* by Conor Cruise O'Brien who accused her of being too close to the nationalist community. But what he really disliked in her was her independence—that she was no hack and followed a story back to the truth and just didn't repeat the establishment line. Not that I always agreed with her. But she had integrity and emotionally was on the side of the underdog.

When Bobby went on hunger strike I think he knew he was going to die. He designed the hunger strike in such a way that when one man died he was replaced by another comrade. It also meant that unlike the 1980 hunger strike, when the men all started the strike together and were all disadvantaged and in a weakened condition when important decisions might have to be taken with regards to offers or negotiations, the 1981 strike would be different. Among the hunger strikers would be men close to death and other participants who would be weak but alert, and they would be advised by the IRA OC Bik McFarlane and by members of the Movement on the outside.

When the MP for Fermanagh and South Tyrone, Frank Maguire, died suddenly and a by-election was called, the decision to put forward Bobby was not taken lightly. The prisoners put forward their arguments in 'comms', which Tom Hartley in the H-Block Office had the foresight to protect and preserve for posterity. We were privy to the thinking of the prisoners and we discussed the proposal at length, at leadership.

People have asked me why I didn't keep a diary of events. We were working flat out but, anyway, we did not write things down because we were constantly being stopped and searched by the guards. If they'd found anything about strategy or plans you can be sure that those would have made their way into the media (and to the Brits) and been twisted around. So we didn't keep an ongoing record.

There were republicans who were not confident Bobby would win. They thought that defeat in these circumstances would not only be fatal but humiliating and profoundly demoralising for years to come, and that blame would fall on those in the leadership (mostly Belfast and Tyrone republicans) who agreed with the intervention. It was a huge risk for everyone—Bobby, the prisoners, the leadership, the overall struggle and the cause.

But there are times when you have to be decisive and bold and this was one of those historic moments.

Although I was convinced that Thatcher would not relent, there was some slight hope after Bobby was elected MP for Fermanagh and South Tyrone. It was an opportunity for Thatcher, if she wanted, to resolve the situation on the basis of his mandate. Thatcher was intransigent. Thatcher, the British and the English in particular have never understood the people in any of their colonies. They misread the situation in Ireland (not for the first time). They could not for one second grasp the strength of conviction and determination and commitment of those young men and young women. Thatcher was heartless, she was sadistic—as we saw again a year later when she ordered the killings of three hundred sailors, mostly teenagers, on the torpedoed *General Belgrano* during the Falklands/Malvinas war when the ship was sailing away from the British exclusion zone around the islands.

Austin Currie of the SDLP—who would later join Fine Gael—threatened to stand against Bobby but was outmaneuvered by our people who let it appear that the late MP Frank Maguire's brother was running. At the last minute Noel Maguire withdrew and Bobby's nomination papers were lodged before the deadline. Years later, Currie as a TD would criticise Michael D Higgins for dropping Section 31 of the Broadcasting Act which banned Sinn Féin from television and radio.

I had met Gerry Fitt in the late 1960s and was not impressed. He played a despicable role during the prison protest. Before he left the SDLP, and before John Hume took over as leader, the SDLP must have known how corrupt he was. The party has completely written him out of their history. In recent years a document was unearthed from Kew Gardens, where British government archives are housed. It was found by the researcher Ciaran Mac Airt, the grandson of a woman killed in McGurk's Bar. It showed that after fifteen of Fitt's neighbours, Catholic children, men and women, were killed in the McGurk's Bar explosion in 1971, he wrote to the British Home Office telling them that the IRA was responsible. The report says, 'He [Gerry Fitt] feels that every effort should be made to pin responsibility for the McGurk's bar explosion on the provisionals.' His reason? It would give the SDLP and 'him an excuse to join discussions' with Brian Faulkner's Ulster Unionist Party. Faulkner had introduced internment just four months earlier and all nationalist parties had pledged not to enter talks until internment was ended.

But worse was to come during the hunger strike.

In the House of Commons, Fitt called upon Thatcher not to give in to the hunger strikers.

On the fifty-fifth day of Bobby's hunger strike and two weeks after he had been elected MP—when hopes, however forlorn, were raised about a compromise—Fitt rang up the NIO seeking further assurances that Thatcher was not going to give into the prisoners. 'I gave him that assurance and he was content,' wrote Jonathan Margetts, a parliamentary secretary.

When Fitt lost his seat to Gerry Adams two years after the hunger strike Thatcher made him a life peer in the House of Lords. Fitt had been bought off long before that. He spent the rest of his days, and there were many, drinking in the bar in Westminster, on a huge pension, wheeled out now and again to attack the working-class people he had deserted. He became the joke Irishman and it was cringe-making. The Brits turned him into a caricature and he let them. During marches the kids use to chant, 'Gerry Fitt is a Brit!' And he was.

One hundred thousand people attended Bobby Sands' funeral in Belfast. Internationally, the Brits were getting hammered—and it wasn't just limited to Irish America. It was in Paris, Amsterdam, Barcelona, Lisbon, India, Australia. Demonstrations were held daily in front of British consulates across the USA. Longshoremen refused to unload British ships on the day of Bobby's funeral. And bus drivers in New York kept their headlights on all day to honour him. The Massachusetts's state senate sent a message of condolences to the Sands' family.

We had moved into our house on Granville Road in October 1980 just as the first hunger strike was beginning. I think we had moved about five times in eight years. We never regretted buying this house but there were times when I thought we would not be able to hang on to it, in the Eighties especially when work was scarce. The responsibility for the big bills and the mortgage fell very much on Brendan. No matter how hard things were, Brendan came up trumps and we paid that mortgage.

There were many people sympathetic to the prisoners but ours was the only house to fly a black flag after Bobby's death. People were afraid—especially of the Special Branch—who were really *political* police. They were bully boys.

We had many people stay with us—from the Troops Out Movement and from solidarity groups in Europe, as well as many republican comrades down for meetings or marches. Ours was an open house. I'm sure hundreds of people stayed with us in those grim times.

I remember many of the marches. I remember seeing huge numbers in Dublin marching out of working-class areas. There's no doubt that something was stirring and that many of these activists would later join the Movement—in a variety of capacities. There were 'Punks Against The H-Blocks', 'Skinheads Against The Blocks' with their own banners. My son Rory and daughter Frances were on the marches. Terry, who later became a typesetter in *An Phoblacht*, was then in Belfast, visiting her future husband Rab McCallum who was on the blanket.

We had a big march in Dún Laoghaire. I'd our Ciaran with me, who was about four then. I remember Deasún Breatnach walking in it.

Deasún, who was a sub-editor at the *Irish Independent* while editor of *An Phoblacht* until it merged with *Republican News* in 1979, could easily have lost his job or work but was undeterred. He'd also helped me move into the council house after Granitefield.

Some of the best coverage and investigative journalism in the 1970s could be read in *Hibernia*, an independent fortnightly magazine, and the early *Sunday Tribune,* both founded by John Mulcahy. Though his later work would me marred by pomposity, self-righteousness and hostility, particularly towards Gerry Adams, Ed Moloney's journalism back then was among the best in terms of what was happening in the North. *The Guardian* often covered the prison protest far better than the press in Ireland. Indeed, its then correspondent, David Beresford, went on to write what many consider to be the most comprehensive account of that prison period, *Ten Men Dead,* though, later, former prisoners wrote extremely moving and intimate memoirs which would make your hair stand on end.

Disgracefully, one year after the hunger strike—but an indication of the battle lines being drawn—the *Irish News* took a decision to ban death notices for Bobby Sands when Bobby's sister, Marcella, went to place an insertion on his anniversary. At the same time the *Irish News* took a decision to carry death notices for RUC officers killed in the conflict.

There were other journalists who knew that the treatment of the prisoners was morally wrong but they, especially those who worked in RTÉ, feared for their positions. They would have marched against apartheid South Africa but not apartheid Six Counties. Members of the Workers Party held huge sway and influence within RTÉ and had created a climate of fear as they ruthlessly enforced Section 31. They, and government watchmen, were always on the alert for anyone who might waiver in their hostility to the Republican Movement or the cause of unity. In 1988, Jenny McGeevor, a freelance reporter on contract to RTÉ, was sacked for interviewing Martin McGuinness as the bodies of the three Volunteers shot in Gibraltar travelled over the border. A furious cabinet minister, Ray Burke, with some hyperbole, told RTÉ that 'the foundations of the state' were shaking. That would be the same state he was fiddling. In 2005 Ray Burke was imprisoned for tax evasion and had also been found corrupt, taking backhanders from developers and businessmen.

For a while there was even a pirate radio station in Dublin broadcasting updates on the hunger strike. Support steadily grew and you could see this in the election of blanket men Kieran Doherty (who would die a few months later) and Paddy Agnew as TDs in the June 1981 general election. But even with the election of Kieran and Paddy—symbolizing thirty-two county republicanism and a breach of partition—I knew that the stakes were so high for the Dublin Government that effectively they would align with British strategy. They would want to turn the hunger strike against the Movement. They viewed the achievement of political status as a victory for republicanism. I think many members of Fianna Fáil were horrified by what was happening. Certainly, people like Síle de Valera and Independent Fianna Fáil TD Neil Blaney made it clear where they stood. But the Irish Establishment was going to protect its interests at all costs—regardless of what disturbances there were—and we can see that same willfulness even today with the resistance to a referendum on Irish unity.

The march to the British Embassy on Merrion Road in July 1981 was huge, about 10,000 strong, some say 20,000. Brendan was at the front but I was further back. It was viciously attacked by the guards who were six deep protecting the embassy. A few missiles had been thrown at their ranks but their response was savage and disproportionate and the attack was clearly premeditated. Escape routes were blocked off and most people were fenced in and not all could escape the violence. There were about 200 people injured, including guards. Many of the injured never reported to hospital for fear of arrest. People of course fought back. They had to, to save others, including mothers and children from being assaulted.

I remember seeing Jack Crowe and Aengus Ó Snodaigh—who are now TDs—being chased. How Aengus wasn't killed is a miracle. I had been separated from Brendan and was looking for him when a guard ran at me and hit me across the arm for no reason. Sonny McStay, a Shinner from Ballymun flats, who was sheltering with me in a doorway, was whacked over the head with a baton. Some shops opened their doors to give us shelter. We could've been people simply waiting for a bus. They just attacked everybody, indiscriminately kicking and beating old men and young girls. People ran across railway lines to escape. Some ran across a cricket pitch, just to get safely away. I remember some of the injured going to a doctor's house for help. He initially wouldn't let anyone in but then relented. He was afraid of the guards seeing him give first aid.

The guards burnt the H-Blocks banners and then, a few miles away, launched an attack on the hunger strike vigil outside the GPO, breaking a man's leg, and tearing up the Book of Condolences for the relatives of Martin Hurson, the sixth hunger striker to die, five days earlier. There were no mobile phones back then. I can't remember how I got home. I think I found Brendan or he found me. People were arrested and prosecuted and sentenced to terms of imprisonment. Others who were seriously injured were afraid to take cases of assault against the guards in case they too would face trumped-up charges.

Some years ago I learnt that there were 200 Irish Army soldiers in the grounds of the embassy with orders to open fire on the demonstrators rather than let the embassy be damaged, as it was in 1972 after Bloody Sunday when it was burnt to the ground.

There was no doubt that the magnitude of the protests was frightening the Southern Government which had decided not to challenge the Brits over its treatment of republican prisoners. It would only be a few years after the burning of the British Embassy that the Fine Gael/Labour coalition government was itself cracking down on the political prisoners in Portlaoise and sanctioning the use of 'the heavy gang', a group of detectives which beat people in custody, extracted false confessions, and was the subject of condemnation from Amnesty International and other human rights bodies. In his memoir Cruise O'Brien admits to having supported Garda Síochána brutality from 1973 to 1977, and said 'it didn't worry me'.

I remember black flags now starting to appear in places where you would never see them, young people wearing Bobby Sands' badges. Places like Ballybrack, among many other places, would have had demonstrations of support and solidarity and that was beginning to really rattle the Dublin Government. There was a colourful and cheery character, well-known in these parts, Bill 'Ubi' Dwyer, who would go around on an old bicycle campaigning for free festivals and the legalisation of cannabis. Ubi was an anarchist activist best known as the originator and principal organiser of the Windsor Free Festival in England in the early 1970s. And now here he was, this popular wee man, cycling around and handing out stickers and petitions in support of the H-Blocks hunger strikers.

The dedication and the commitment of the hunger strikers was not only astonishing at the time but you can see that when the conflict is viewed as a whole, or bracketed say between 1968 and 1998, then the year 1981 'thunders forth its might', as Bobby Sands wrote in his poem, *The Rhythm of Time*. Bobby was only twenty-seven. Thomas McElwee, twenty-three.

The 1981 hunger strike, the immense suffering and sacrifices behind it and the protests in Armagh and the H-Blocks, were transformative, the effects long-lasting. Just as the deaths of Thomas Ashe in 1917 and Terence Mac Swiney in 1920 had a profound effect, I'd say that the deaths of those ten blanket men were the catalyst for all the changes that eventually led to the rise of Sinn Féin as the most powerful political force in contemporary Irish national politics.

There had been earlier electoral interventions when prisoners had stood and been elected in the 1950s: Ruairí Ó Brádaigh (Roscommon); John Joe McGirl (Leitrim); Tom Mitchell (Mid-Ulster); and Phil Clarke (Fermanagh and South Tyrone). These elections were significant and showed support and sympathy for republicanism but politically were not on the Richter scale of 1981 which gave birth to the Movement we see today.

Over my lifetime I have been amazed at how often so-called intelligent political commentators, academics and historians get things wrong. A notion is created, takes root and becomes the orthodoxy. For example, the Sticks (the 'Official IRA') from the time of the split in 1969/1970 projected an image of themselves as radical and internationalist, whereas we were depicted as insular, right-wing Catholics, created by Fianna Fáil and other dark forces to thwart the coming revolution of 'workers and small farmers'. It could also be seen when pen-portraits of our republican leaders appeared in the media: almost all were 'daily communicants'—which was code for 'reactionary'. Some were even described as 'teetotal'—signal for being bores and not good company!

The fact is that life on the ground dictated what the priorities were at any specific time. After 1969 it was the defence of those vulnerable working-class areas where the nationalist community was most densely concentrated. It was about securing arms, smuggling them in, hiding them and getting people trained in their use. Later, it became open resistance and then armed struggle. So, while Sinn Féin existed, and was, like the IRA, a proscribed organisation, though not as 'underground', so to speak, it was not extensively organized and was perceived as secondary in the Republican Movement partnership, even though it was often the public face of protest and its members suffered great harassment. The antipathy to and lack of enthusiasm for elections was based less on organisational shortcomings or self-confidence or lack of candidates than on historical analysis—that Britain would ignore results that didn't suit its imperial purpose. From 1969, given the intensities, there were greater priorities for our limited material resources. So, while our absence from elections allowed the Sticks to strut the stage with their hollow rhetoric (revisionism disguised as a revolutionary platform) and gave the emergent SDLP a monopoly on the nationalist vote, our struggle continued afoot. In the prisons republicans generated ideas, explored strategies and possibilities, and devoted themselves to education and study which would later bear fruit—seen also in the rise of the movement demanding Irish language rights.

CHAPTER EIGHT

THE BRUTAL 1980s

Owen Carron, a member of Sinn Féin, had been elected MP in the second Fermanagh and South Tyrone by-election in August 1981. He had been Bobby Sands' election agent but Thatcher had brought in a new law banning prisoners from participating in elections, which is why Owen was put forward and not a hunger striker. (In a law of unintended consequences Thatcher's actions ironically facilitated our adoption of an electoral strategy.) Owen had been elected on an anti-H-Block/Armagh ticket but after the end of the hunger strike in October 1981 he sat as a Sinn Féin abstentionist MP and now used his election campaign offices in Enniskillen and Dungannon as constituency advice centres.

There were many arguments against taking part in elections. You could lose and would unnecessarily demoralise the base and hand your opponents another stick to beat you with—that is, that you had no mandate. Elections would involve a huge drain on resources and personnel—and Sinn Féin at this time was basically a protest and campaigning movement. Though we had some councillors in the South our rules barred us from participating and taking seats in the northern councils which is why in the May elections in 1981 it was the Irish Independence Party, the Irish Republican Socialist Party and People's Democracy who won seats. Another argument against participation was that the Brits simply ignored election victories which they disliked. Finally, there was the danger that an electoral strategy would come to predominate and preoccupy the Movement before the IRA's armed struggle had created the breakthrough conditions for peace and progress, including a declaration by Britain that it would recognise the right of the Irish people to national self-determination.

The advantages, however, in my opinion, were overwhelming.

Bobby Sands becoming an MP had exposed British propaganda and destroyed their programme of criminalisation here and on the international stage with the likes of the *New York Times* now referring to the IRA as guerrilla fighters. Election successes would curb the SDLP and its disastrous policies and force them onto a more nationalist path. Election successes would insulate the struggle. The election of Paddy Agnew and Kieran Doherty hurt Fianna Fáil and inaugurated the era of fraught coalition governments in the South. Being elected also meant that as representatives we could give something (a dedicated constituency service) back to the people who had borne the weight of the struggle—which had gone on for far longer than anyone anticipated in the early days.

At the 1981 Ard Fheis, just a month after the ending of the hunger striker, the ard comhairle put forward a motion seeking approval for participation on an abstentionist basis in a future Stormont Assembly election which the new Secretary of State James Prior was advancing. But during the debate surprising numbers spoke against the proposal for a variety of reasons—many stating that it was 'a slippery slope' to constitutional politics and ending abstentionism towards Leinster House, Stormont and Westminster. Some of these speakers would split from Sinn Féin five years later. It was at this point that Danny Morrison made his 'Armalite and Ballot Box' speech and the motion was passed.

In the 1982 assembly elections in the North the party contested several seats, won five, and received 10% of first preference votes. It was a major shock to the media that had ignored Sinn Féin during the campaign and had predicted a derisory 3% result. Recently, an opinion poll in the North put Sinn Féin on 32%, as the largest party in the Six Counties, to the SDLP's 7%.

That 10% we received really rattled our opponents, particularly the British and Irish governments. There was republican support out there beyond the base we usually relied upon. In the Westminster general election in 1983 our vote increased and Gerry Adams took Fitt's seat in West Belfast.

One month later Belfast City Council, that jewel of unionism, was changed utterly. It's probably hard for young people to understand—given that we are so used to elections now—the excitement I felt when Alex Maskey was elected as the first Sinn Féin councillor in Belfast to that bastion of sectarianism. That was the chink in the dam. I remember when Belfast city centre was really a no-go area for us. In the old days, when you got off the train you got out of there fast.

Alex was booed and jeered as he entered the chamber. It got worse. He was punched, kicked, spat on, wasn't allowed to speak, was drowned out by Paisley's daughter Rhonda and Sammy Wilson blowing whistles and horns. Isn't it interesting that RTÉ, while exercising Section 31 against us, allowed the same Rhonda Paisley to guest host a television episode of 'Saturday Live' in which her main guest was, yes, her father. One unionist councillor tried to spray Alex with disinfectant, stating that the chamber needed sanitised. In 1987, Alex was shot and seriously wounded at his home. On another occasion his house was again attacked and his friend Alan Lundy was shot dead.

Alex was tough. A former boxer. At subsequent elections he was joined by Sean McKnight, Máirtín Ó Muilleoir, Lily Fitzsimons, Tish Holland (another former Armagh prisoner) and Fra McCann—wee Fra—and others. He became Lord Mayor of Belfast. Veteran republican Marie Moore—in whose house Tom Williams was shot and arrested in 1942, and who was later hanged—became the first Sinn Féin Deputy Mayor. Today, Sinn Féin is the largest party on Belfast City Council and Alex is the Speaker in the Assembly in what was once the unionist citadel of Stormont.

Although prisoner candidates in the June 1981 general election in the South did exceptionally well, Sinn Féin was not able to repeat that success when we stood for election in February 1982. The post mortem on those results inevitably led to a questioning of the abstentionist policy towards Leinster House—that the electorate in the South expected you to take your seats and represent them. I'd say most of the discussions were in private, among friends. I can't remember if we aired them in the letters page of *An Phoblacht/Republican News* but I don't think we did. At least, not at that stage.

One of the reasons for the republican split in 1969/1970 included proposals to end abstentionism towards all three parliaments—Westminster, Stormont and Leinster House. At that time, Stormont, a unionist government in perpetuity, epitomised nationalist second-class status and was an anathema. You could not change the unionist mindset of supremacy by indulging it. It would take thirty years to chasten the DUP and force them—kicking and screaming—into power-sharing with Sinn Féin. The Stormont experiment remains a work-in-progress, a station along the way, because everything confirms the republican analysis that the Six Counties is an irreconcilable political entity.

Abstentionism from Leinster House went back to the dreadful Civil War which saw republicans defeated, the people deeply divided, and northern nationalists abandoned. Abstentionism was aimed at denying the legitimacy of the British-established Southern state. Fianna Fáil was formed by de Valera and split from Sinn Féin with the alleged purpose of entering Leinster House to repudiate and roll back the 1921 Treaty. However, the party quickly identified solely with the Twenty-Six Counties and it too became as partitionist as Cumann na nGaedheal and Fine Gael.

Entering Leinster House was a red line for people like Ruairí and Dave. They had gone to extraordinary lengths to copper-fasten abstentionism, inserting it in the party's constitution which meant it required a two-thirds majority at an Ard Fheis just to *discuss* it. My friend Kathleen Knowles' father and two uncles, I think, had suffered for the republican cause before and after the Civil War and she found it unconscionable to take seats in Leinster House. So the subject had to be approached with care and sensitivity and an appeal to comradeship and the survival of the struggle.

Another major obstacle was that it had also been embedded in the IRA's constitution. Despite the argument that the IRA, for its own survival, had changed policy and adopted a pragmatic approach, giving Volunteers permission to recognise the courts and fight cases that could be won, resulting in their release to fight another day, Ruairí and Dave were having none of it. Dave even stated that if he were charged with IRA membership he would still refuse to recognise the court. A principled stance but one which would lead to an extra burden of work on others while he served his sentence.

Abstentionism from Westminster was clear-cut, having been adapted after the December general election in 1918 when Sinn Féin swept the boards and established Dáil Éireann. There is no way I would ever countenance the taking of seats there—and not just because it requires the taking of an oath of loyalty to the British monarch. There are principles you can never compromise on and this is one. Westminster is a foreign parliament and given that it has no moral right to be interfering in our affairs, we would have no moral right to sit there and interfere in its affairs. Taking seats there would never result in Irish independence and the end of British rule in our country. The majority of nationalists agree with that policy and vote overwhelmingly for abstentionist Sinn Féin MPs.

So, we had to adapt to certain realities and one was that people in the Twenty-Six Counties identified with the institutions of the state and the seat of parliament, Leinster House. They considered them legitimate. To be relevant we would have to end abstentionism—which was not an easy thing, especially emotionally given the way republicans had been mistreated in the South. Ruairí and Dave viewed electoral intervention in terms of a single issue—to prove a point. For example, that there was support for a hunger strike and political status. You participate. You win. You walk away. We viewed it in a more revolutionary way, of involving people, raising morale, representing people in their everyday struggles, undermining the propaganda of our opponents, building an alternative leadership to establishment parties, challenging authority.

There were other changes in policy which had alienated Ruairí and Dave. At the 1983 Ard Fheis Dave resigned as vice-president of Sinn Féin after the party abandoned *Éire Nua*, with its plan for four federal provincial assemblies. Often, anything we did caused suspicion, especially if it involved broadening our policy.

We had battles before when we set up the Women's Department in 1980. I won't remember all of the names but the women involved included: Martha McClelland, Daisy Mules, Sheila Fanning, Marie Mulholland, Maura McCrory, Chrissie McAuley, and Lucilita Bhreatnach. There were also Women's Department committees in Derry, Dublin, Belfast and other places. Resistance to this wasn't exactly a left-right divide but some in leadership viewed it as a challenge and some older members were fairly set in their ways.

Sinn Féin, just like the vast majority of other political parties around the world, was male-dominated. There *were* women on the ard comhairle but we were few and far between and our numbers didn't reflect the amount of women who were active both in the IRA and in the party, their ability and their revolutionary determination and enthusiasm. There was change coming in society here, and we could not be outside that. But it had to be discussed and, incredibly looking back now, many had to be won over.

I remember daft things; I remember the first Ard Fheis when women's rights were on the clar. Subjects down for debate were violence against women and another about women standing for election within Sinn Féin, never mind being chosen for candidates for elections! Some old man stood up and said, 'The next thing youse'll want is free love on the buses!' And, of course, many, many clapped and cheered him and laughed at his observation which casually they might have thought harmless but it underpinned a deep-rooted chauvinism. That anyone thought his contribution was of value showed how far we still had to go.

I also remember women *opposing* there being talk about women's rights. I remember one of the older women saying, not just to me because we invited all members to start talking about it, but one said, pointing to the ard chomhairle on the platform, 'What do you want now, to be up there?'

I said, 'Yeh, that's exactly what we want. Half the population are women. We have to show that we represent them, or at least make an attempt.'

A century ago Countess Markievicz spoke of the three great movements in Ireland: the national movement, the labour movement and the women's movement. All three converged in 1916 in one fateful attempt to achieve the dominant goal—national freedom. Afterwards, they were to drift apart on separate roads. It became the responsibility of our struggle to re-link these three strands. Within the Movement some republicans could be smug and conceited, convinced that there was no bar or restrictions on women reaching positions of seniority. In theory, yes; but in practice our ranks were male-dominated and many men were not even aware of their sexist attitudes, which, of course, was reflective of the prevailing culture in Irish life and political life.

The heroism of the women of Cumann na mBan in 1916 and through the Tan War is indisputable. However, their role was not the same as an IRA Volunteer's role. Cumann na mBan concentrated on such duties as scouting, despatch-carrying, intelligence work and first aid. Their role was a vital one but Markievicz herself criticised this role as being primarily a back-up one, and it was in the ranks of the Irish Citizen Army that she fought in St Stephen's Green in 1916.

From the early 1970s until the ceasefire many women fought side-by-side on IRA operations with their male comrades. In jail they suffered in the fight for political status. It used to drive me mad the way republican speakers would refer to 'the girls' in Armagh, rather than 'the women'. Was it because 'girls' can be allowed the wild impetuosity of becoming involved in the military struggle, whilst once they became 'women' they must settle back into their appointed roles as wives, mothers and other more subservient, auxiliary roles, dictated by the norms of male-dominated society? Because of the indoctrination of all of us, the idea of 'grey-haired old ladies' or 'middle-aged mothers' as leaders of the struggle appeared incongruous. Yet, the concept of 'white-haired old gentlemen' in the same role had been almost a point of honour over the years.

The differences between the setting up of the Women's Department in 1980 and attitudes today are incredible, and not just within Sinn Féin.

I'm talking about the changed attitudes in the North to women and to the LGBT community. I'm talking about the fact that the iron stranglehold by partitionists in the South has been broken and that a variety of voices, which along with republicans would have once been muted—people like Joe Brolly and Bernadette McAliskey—can speak about their experiences of sectarianism, discrimination, racism and sexism. Their voices have been a wake-up call for many.

Breakthroughs can be seen everywhere. Films and dramas being made about the struggle, the documentaries. Sean Murray's film, *Unquiet Graves*, highlighting collusion and the killings by the Glenanne Gang, made up of serving members of the RUC, British soldiers and loyalist paramilitaries, was powerful. Even RTÉ was eventually forced to broadcast it, despite repeatedly postponing it. Though there is still a pervasive air of entitlement among the central personalities within RTÉ, gone are the days when the Workers Party through the likes of Eoghan Harris policed and controlled content. It was disgraceful what went on. The denial of information, the persistent anti-republican bias and the distortion of the truth about the conflict, prolonged that conflict by comforting the British that they would militarily prevail over the nationalist community.

Not that long ago, our Naoise, who is thirty-six, saw an RTÉ programme about the 1981 hunger strike and was asking questions. I gave him a copy of *Ten Men Dead* to read and he came back really angry, asking why he didn't know all this. I said, because you weren't even born. This wasn't a house where we shoved politics down our kids' throats. I mean, they're all republican, but we mostly let them find and decide their own opinions and come to their own understanding, their own conclusions.

I am writing this but my energy levels and concentration often fall and fail me. But as I write I've been listening to music by Kneecap, a Belfast rap group. My granddaughter Sinéad and Liam Óg (Mo Chara in the band) have been together as a couple for several years. I *love* Kneecap's music which is rebellious, political, subversive, highly original and something of a cultural phenomenon. Mary Lou is a big fan, as well! Kneecap emerged from the Irish language movement in Belfast in protest at the denial of Irish language rights, despite the pledges in the Good Friday Agreement and the St Andrew's Agreement. They have a huge following, nationally and internationally. It has been amazing for me to witness all these changes: the confidence of our people, their talent, the Féile in West Belfast, our young ones educated, every professional position open to our people, discrimination (which was the foundation of the six-county state) overturned, no going back: it's over.

When abstentionism towards Leinster House was abandoned at the 1986 Ard Fheis, Ruairí and Dave and their followers walked out and formed Republican Sinn Féin. I was sorry to see some old friends leave, especially Kathleen Knowles. It was a very hard time. It was just that we had to make hard decisions if we were to progress. Thankfully, Kathleen and I were too good friends to stop not being friends. We just agreed to disagree over those aspects of struggle. We remained friends until she died in 2012.

I am not sure how long in the short term we thought it would take before we would make a breakthrough in the South, but it took a long time. Eleven years, in fact. And it came with the election of Caoimhghín Ó Caoláin.

Election of Caoimhghín Ó Caoláin, 1997

During the hunger strike some of the editions of the paper had ran to over eighty-four pages, maybe even more. There was also some inherited debt from having had to keep *Republican News* afloat until the merger. And we were also owed money by many cumainn who had ploughed their commission and sales revenue into local activity! We badly needed a business manager and the man approached by Gerry and Martin for the role was Caoimhghín Ó Caoláin. Mild-mannered and undemonstrative, he had played a key role as Kieran Doherty's director of elections in Cavan/Monaghan and later gave the oration in Milltown Cemetery at Kieran's funeral. He worked in banking and he gave up a career which promised senior promotion and financial security to join the comrades at *An Phoblacht/Republican News*. He absolutely turned the situation around, placing not just the newspaper but Republican Publications which published pamphlets and posters, in the black.

I became a huge admirer of Caoimhghín. I remember being in Monaghan town for a meeting. It was in the advice centre/office established by Caoimhghín. Some of these places were run on a shoestring, could be cramped and chaotic. I looked through the window which displayed a Tricolour and a variety of recently published books. I went in and there was a reception and the place was warm, neat and tidy. Professional. And I remember thinking, this is how you do it. It might have been a small thing but this is how you present your face to the public, be inviting, be friendly and professional, be trained up on housing and employment issues, or taboo subjects like domestic violence and abuse. Work harder than anyone else, any of the other parties. That's how to make a breakthrough. Commit yourself to people and do your best to ameliorate their hardships and their battles against authority and the system. I was absolutely impressed.

I think it was Pádraigín Uí Mhurchadha who was staffing the office. You could see that she loved and enjoyed her work. Pádraigín was the sister of IRA Volunteer Fergal O'Hanlon who with Seán South had been killed during an attack on Brookeborough RUC barracks on New Year's Day 1957 as part of Operation Harvest. Caoimhghín had people of great integrity around him to whom the community looked up. In 1985 Pádraigín, Pat Treanor and Owen Smith were all elected to Monaghan Town Council and Caoimhghín to Monaghan County Council.

Sinn Féin's profile was largely associated with the national question, opposition to state repression, republican causes around prisoners, the organisation of commemorations and events at Easter, and the promotion of the Irish language. But we were also increasingly involved in a wider range of activism: supporting striking workers and pickets, campaigning for human rights and opposition to unjust laws.

We supported and gave extensive coverage to the stance of the Dunnes Stores' workers who for following union guidance and refusing to handle produce from apartheid South Africa were suspended indefinitely before being joined by striking co-workers, nine women and one man in total. Theirs was a principled, moral protest. There were attempts to intimidate and isolate them. Politicians accused them of 'damaging Ireland's reputation'. John Bruton, who as Fine Gael leader, later played such a disastrous role in the peace process, said he was opposed to restricting imports from South Africa. The strike cost the protestors dearly in lost wages for three years, from 1984 until 1987. But they won and the South became the first state in the EU to ban South African imports. Nelson Mandela, when we met him years later, referred to how important and symbolic that strike was, which really demonstrates the power of international solidarity though you might not appreciate it at the time.

In the 1970s and 1980s (but more intensely in the 1990s) there was a huge mobilisation by local communities and farmers to reopen the hundreds of border roads that had been cratered and bridges that had been blown up by the Brits. Protestors were met by rubber bullets, CS gas and baton charges and the Brits would return and blast the roads with even deeper craters. I remember one farmer whose land was in Cavan and Fermanagh who in order to get to his cattle had to complete a sixty-mile round trip. After the ceasefire these roads were all reopened and the bridges repaired, mostly as a result of European peace money. One of the reasons the DUP rejected all compromises and held out for the most extreme form of Brexit was because they anticipated the return of a hard border which would have reinforced partition, physically and psychologically, and demoralised nationalists.

Beginning in Dublin's inner city in the early 1980s we supported the Concerned Parents Against Drugs. Kids as young as fifteen were hooked on heroin. Christy Burke, then a Sinn Féin councillor, sat on the first committee, I think. The problem was at its worse in poor working-class areas of high unemployment where there was a sense of hopelessness.

But pride and a sense of purpose came into the communities who would march on the homes of known drug dealers and demand that they stop destroying families. It was terrific to see people coming out—ordinary people, men, women, kids, on these big marches. They met with huge intimidation and threats from armed gangs. The communities then turned to republicans and put huge pressure on the IRA to become involved—which would have been disastrous, though the IRA was accused of it anyway. The guards seemed more concerned about crushing 'people power' than the drug barons who attacked the homes and cars of activists and Sinn Féin members. Many arrests were made and, disgracefully, community activists were subjected to prosecutions in the non-jury Special Criminal Court, rather than the District Court. In one case the guards called as prosecution witnesses three known drug dealers.

I remember going to a meeting with my friend, Kevin Fitzpatrick. We were walking down this street of small houses, that still had outside toilets in the backyard, and Kevin said, 'Watch this.' A van drew up and a crowd of mainly young fellas gathered to collect their supply. They were openly dealing. I said to Kevin. 'Do the Guards not see this?' He said, 'Of course they do, but they won't do anything about it.'

Kevin was one of the speakers at the meeting but Barry Desmond, who was a Labour Party TD for the area, wouldn't participate because Kevin was on the platform. However, Desmond then went to a meeting of 'the nice people' up in Foxrock church where he spoke. We went there and challenged him.

I remember Kevin being arrested. The guards deliberately put him into a cell in the Bridewell with a drug dealer, hoping that the criminal would give Kevin a good thrashing.

As I said, Caoimhghín Ó Caoláin became the first member of Sinn Féin to take his seat in Leinster House, in June 1997—at a time when the IRA had resumed its campaign. Although the IRA had cease fired in August 1994, the British Government (supported by Fine Gael Taoiseach John Bruton) and the unionists, had dragged their heels, slowed down talks and substantive negotiations, excluded Sinn Féin, and made demands which had never been mentioned in the secret talks with the IRA which led up to the ceasefire. Caoimhghín, on his own in Leinster House, courageously defended and explained the republican position.

The 1980s were brutal years. The IRA had emerged from 1981 with unbelievable stamina, a huge increase in sympathy, supporters and recruits. It continued its attacks across the North, with other attacks in Britain and in Europe. Thatcher's stupidity in suggesting that the hunger strike was 'the IRA's last card' would come back to imperil her.

The war could be ugly, certain IRA operations demoralising and dispiriting, but the prevailing republican opinion was that there was no way out until a tipping point was reached. It would require great and careful and cautious judgement appreciating when you had arrived at the point when politics exclusively became a viable alternative to conflict.

Britain deployed every tactic possible to defeat republicans and its supporters. Thirty-thousand plastic bullets were fired in 1981 alone, their targets not just demonstrators but innocent people, including children.

The first child to be killed in the Troubles was nine-year-old Patrick Rooney, killed by the RUC who opened fire with heavy machineguns in August 1969 into Divis Flats. Six years later, in that same area, the British Army shot dead ten-year-old Stephen Geddis with a rubber bullet.

The Brits and their courts were modified—as advocated by counter-insurgency theorist Brigadier Frank Kitson—to literally stamp convictions regardless, and used Supergrasses and Show Trials until this strategy was brought completely into disrepute. There were shoot-to-kill operations by the British Army and RUC against unarmed republicans. There were attacks on republican funerals. There was the arming of loyalist paramilitaries by British Intelligence who had oversight of, and helped direct their attacks. The British Army, RUC and UDR colluded with loyalist murder gangs who killed hundreds of innocent Catholics. The loyalists, who claimed to have been fighting 'a war', never once took on or confronted an armed republican but carried out gun and bomb attacks on republicans, their homes and their families. The assassinations of elected representatives and Sinn Féin activists included the attempt to kill Gerry Adams in 1984 which resulted in him being severely wounded along with several other comrades. There were the killings and threats to kill those in the legal profession. There was censorship via the British Broadcasting Ban. There was the restriction of movements under Exclusion Orders which barred republican speakers on pain of imprisonment from entering Britain.

Later, there was the assassination of Larry Marley with the mourners being baton-charged every time his coffin was being taken from his home for burial. There were other disgraceful scenes with the coffin of a Volunteer in Derry crashing to the ground after pall bearers were beaten by the RUC. There were the SAS killings of nine at Loughgall—eight Volunteers and a civilian. The first time the RUC and British Army stayed back from a funeral was at the burial in Milltown Cemetery of the three West Belfast republicans killed in Gibraltar—Mairéad Farrell, Sean Savage and Dan McCann. That funeral was attacked by loyalist assassin Michael Stone, armed with weapons delivered to Ian Paisley's

Ulster Resistance, the UDA and the UVF with the help of British Intelligence and apartheid South Africa.

Three people were killed: IRA Volunteer Kevin Brady, and civilians Thomas McErlean and John Murray who were both married. The funeral of Kevin Brady, a few days later, was disrupted by a car driving at high speed towards mourners. Everyone present believed it was another loyalist attack—even a radio journalist broadcast a newsflash saying exactly that. It turned out that the two in the car were British soldiers in plainclothes, armed with Browning pistols. Stewards on the Andersonstown Road were directing traffic into side streets but they ignored them and accelerated toward the funeral. To this day the British MoD has never explained why they were there and what they were doing.

Their capture by the crowd and their killing by the IRA made for horrific images which were transmitted around the world, depicting the republican community as savages. It was truly a terrible time, coming just months after the Enniskillen bombing by the IRA on Remembrance Sunday in which eleven people were killed.

The British Government and republican opponents demonised not just republicans but the community they came from. It was sheer hypocrisy, a double standard, and omitted those who initiated the conflict against this community.

And yet, their pogroms, the Falls Curfew, internment, Bloody Sunday, and the relentless oppression all ignominiously failed. It only made republicans more determined to continue. To have ended the conflict in any other circumstances than it eventually did would have only taken the pressure off the British and made them complacent, would have reinforced unionist intransigence and belligerence, would have left both Sinn Féin and the SDLP impotent, and would have suited the Irish Establishment which feared its interests being compromised. (In fact, the eventual IRA ceasefire of August 1994 would be taken for granted and resulted in the IRA resuming a limited campaign with the bombing of London's Canary Wharf in 1996.)

The Brits could also be inexplicably stupid. For example, in 1982 the governor of Armagh Jail introduced strip-searching—which was disproportionately applied to political prisoners—after two young non-republican prisoners were found in possession of keys that they had picked up in a courthouse.

All female prisoners over the age of fifteen were to be strip-searched regardless if they were having their period, returning from hospital or were pregnant. Jacqueline Moore was strip-searched after giving birth and she and her baby Dominque were subjected to constant body searches. Martina Anderson, Ella O'Dwyer and Martina Shanahan, republican prisoners in English jails were also subjected to numerous searches. Despite being under 24-hour surveillance Ella and Martina were strip-searched over 400 times in one fourteen-month period.

Brendan's sister Briege, who served six years in Armagh, was one of those affected. Republican women often spent three years awaiting trial but they were stripped naked before and after each remand hearing. The Dublin psychologist Dr Ivor Browne compared strip searching to rape—an act of violence and hatred.

Despite condemnation of the practice and the bad publicity it incurred, nationally and internationally, the British obstinately continued with the policy, one they had not even introduced for male prisoners in the H-Blocks after the great escape of 1983. After thousands of strip searches the practice was eventually ended after three years without any credible explanation for the change in policy.

On 26 January 1985 we heard the sad news that Mick Timothy died after a fall at this home, though I think the cause of death was heart disease. Mick had been editor of *An Phoblacht/Republican News* since October 1982.

I was now asked to become editor.

Official opening of Teach Mick Timothy, 58 Parnell Square, Dublin, January 1988. Next to Rita, Mick's children and their mother, Alice

Despite now having elected representatives in the North, Sinn Féin was excluded from the New Ireland Forum, established in 1983 by Fine Gael Taoiseach Garret Fitzgerald. Unionist parties, who all supported state violence and excused loyalist violence, were invited but snubbed it. We believed at the time, and it was confirmed subsequently, that this was Fitzgerald's attempt to help the SDLP whose monopoly on the nationalist vote now faced electoral competition from republicans. Its report was published in 1984, just in time for the European elections in which John Hume stood again.

At a press conference, Thatcher famously rejected the Forum's three proposals—a unitary state, a federal/confederal state, and joint British/Irish authority—summarised by her remarks, 'Out', 'Out', 'Out'. Nevertheless, work continued privately between Irish and British civil servants and it resulted in the (Hillsborough) Anglo-Irish Agreement in 1985. In return for some favour the South pledged ever-greater security cooperation and to smooth the process of extradition of republicans, that is, to withdraw the political motivation exemption. Several republicans were subsequently extradited, including Dessie Ellis to England but he was acquitted at trial. Dessie is now a Dublin TD.

John Hume was a very inspiring speaker, no doubt about that, and he absolutely, definitely changed things, particularly for Derry. He was doing good work for the people of Derry even before the peace process. Seamus Mallon was also an articulate speaker but he was no republican. His rhetoric about wanting Irish unity was exposed as just that, rhetoric. In fact, just before he died he repudiated the criterion in the Good Friday Agreement which states that a simple majority (the basis for the North remaining in the union) would be enough to carry a constitutional referendum on Irish unity. This was music to the ears of unionists and the leaders of Fianna Fáil and Fine Gael. Mallon's way would be to gerrymander the single constituency of the Six Counties in favour of a unionist minority.

I know for a fact the Department of Foreign Affairs crafted speeches for the SDLP. The relationship between the Irish Establishment and the SDLP was inimical to the cause of reunification. They wanted partition to work, for the North not to be abolished but to be stabilised with social democratic norms (which proved elusive), and with the least amount of disruption to the sanctimonious South. In some of the state papers, released under the twenty- or thirty-year rule, you can see the SDLP telling Dublin what it wants to hear about republicans. They saw the IRA campaign as the problem and not the British military campaign in support of partition.

The electoral rise and success of Sinn Féin has absolutely changed the situation because it represented for the first time in a long time the possibility of real change.

Portrait of Rita by Brendan Brownlee, 2024

FAMILY, FRIENDS AND COMRADES

Aodhán, Terry, Sinéad, Rita, Gerry, Caolain, Aoife, Frances, Rory,
Killiney Castle, 2022

Terry, Rita, Rory and Frances, 1971

Rita and Margaret Gatt with Carmen, Ciaran and Porky, 1979

Maureen, Rita's mother who died in December 1996

Billy, Rita's father who died in May 2003

At home with (great granddaughter) Keelin, and Laura

Christmas with (just some) of the children

From left: Naoise, Joanne, Luiseach, Rioghnach, Cathal, Oisín, Rab, Kevin, Brendan. From right: Aoife, Patrick, Fionntan, Christine, Terry, Rita

With her brother, Alan

With Seán McManus, Ard Comhairle

With staff and former staff of *An Phoblach/Republican News* at the opening of
Teach Mick Timothy, January 1988

Mick Timothy

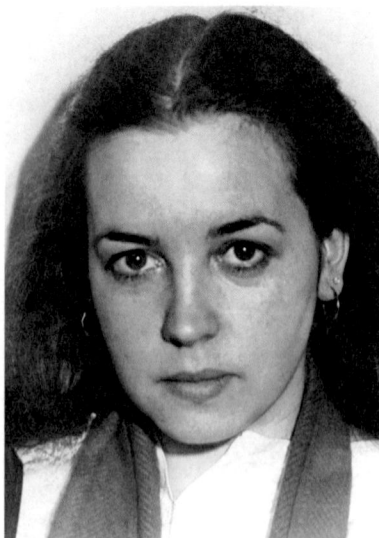

Siobhán O'Hanlon

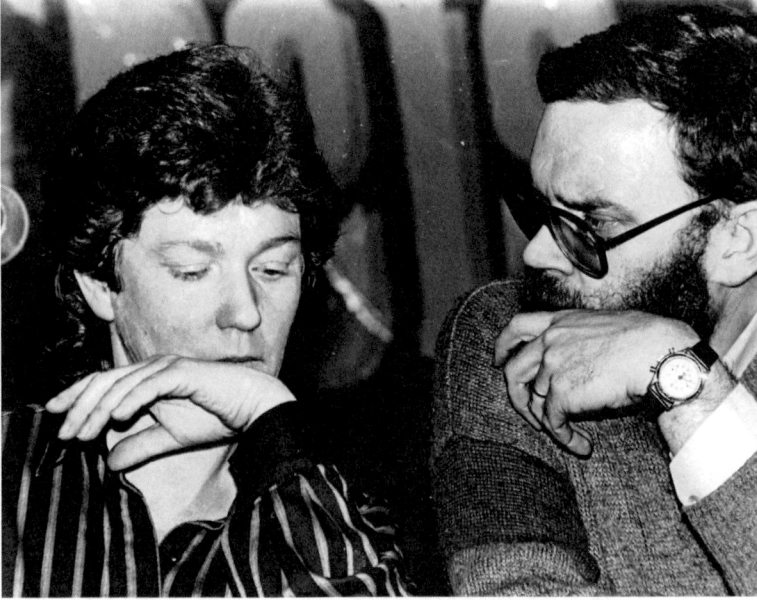

With Tom Hartley, General Secretary Sinn Féin

With Pat Doherty MP, Vice-President Sinn Féin

With Jim Gibney and Terence 'Cleeky' Clarke (just behind Gerry), outside
Government Buildings, Dublin, 1994

With Richard McAuley, Pat Doherty, Gerry, Martin and Lucilita, 1995

'Conspiring' with Martin Ferris, Sinn Féin TD

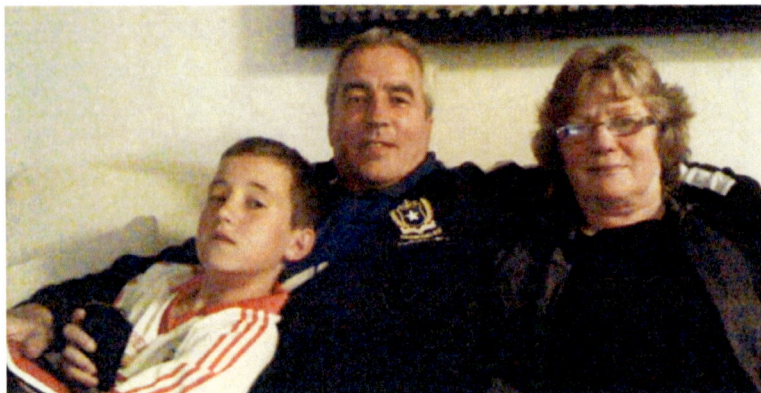

With Cormac and Pat Sheehan

With Ruan O'Donnell (historian), Fionnuala Flanagan, Gerry and Bobby Ballagh, San Franscisco conference, April 2009

With Lily Hall and Annie Cahill, wife of Joe Cahill, at the 2009 Árd Fheis

With Michelle O'Neill, Vice-President Sinn Féin

Brendan with Joseph
Smith and Ciaran Quinn
Killiney Castle, 2022

With Danny Morrison, Síle Darragh and
Tim Pat Coogan, July 2022

With Joseph Smith,
Killiney Castle, 2022

With Gerry in New York, September 2009

CHAPTER NINE

TOWARDS PEACE

Early in 1990 Danny Morrison was arrested in Belfast and charged with a number of offences, including conspiracy to kill a police informer and IRA membership. Given the corrupt nature of the Diplock Courts and the resources put into his prosecution it was obvious that he was going to be convicted and imprisoned for some time. Indeed, he was sentenced to eight years. It would be eighteen years before his conviction was overturned on foot of evidence that the *real* conspiracy was that he had been set-up for arrest by an agent, Freddie Scappaticci, working for British Intelligence.

I was now asked to replace Danny as the National Director of Publicity for Sinn Féin. Every job I got was because somebody died, fucked up, or went to jail. They called me the 'fire brigade'. I relinquished my position as editor of *AP/RN* to Mícheál Mac Donncha, one of those young Dublin activists politicised by the hunger strike. Mícheál had joined the party as a student in UCD in 1982 and had been working for the paper since 1985 and was a very good writer.

I was sorry to leave, even though I would still have overall responsibility for the paper as part of my brief. But given that the mainspring of change—back then, anyhow—was the struggle in the North, I felt it would be better served by a publicity director based there and not by someone who couldn't even travel beyond Dundalk! Regardless, I was in my new role on the ard comhairle where national strategy was formulated and where we discussed ongoing political developments.

During the time I was editor, and then Director of Publicity, there were almost fifty IRA Volunteers killed leading up to the peace process. At the same time, it was republicans who were overwhelmingly demonised in the media. One of those killed was Joe McManus, son of dear friends of mine, Helen and Seán McManus from Sligo. Joe was just twenty-one. Later, Seán, who was on the party's negotiating team, was part of

Volunteer Joe McManus

the first Sinn Féin delegation to meet with the British Government in over seventy years. Seán and Helen had one other son, Chris, three years younger than Joe, and who became a Sinn Féin elected representative.

Joe had been part of an IRA active service unit and was fatally wounded in Fermanagh during an exchange of fire with a UDR man near Belleek in February 1992. I had heard that a Volunteer had been shot dead and that he was from Sligo but it wasn't until I got through on the phone and Helen answered that I learnt the devastating news.

We drove to Sligo. There were roadblocks all around the house, on the road from Sligo town and on the back road. Helen, Seán and Chris met me at the door. They were, of course, heartbroken but calm and determined that Joe would be buried with dignity and respect.

Joe's body was to be brought across the border at Blacklion. I waited with a big crowd of republicans at the bridge. It was a dark, sombre night. There was silence as the hearse came in sight—total silence, in my memory—in spite of the throng of people and the huge number of RUC and British soldiers on the other side of the border and the Gardaí on the southern side. Helen wanted Joe home so he was brought directly to the house where his coffin was flanked by an IRA guard of honour.

119

Funeral of Joe McManus. Helen (fourth from right);
Sean (third from right)

Hundreds of people from across Ireland flocked to the wake to pay their respects and condole with the family. I remember Chris and I at one point leaving the house to walk down to the shop for cigarettes and me running back to talk to the person receiving visitors and monitoring the phone.

I said, 'Don't let Seán or Helen answer the phone. Screen all calls.' Because, sadly, there were some bad calls, hate calls, though they were far outweighed by the calls from those offering sympathy and support. Chris and I talked as we walked, and for someone so young and in grief he was remarkably calm and his chief concern was for his parents.

Gerry and Colette Adams arrived early the next morning, with Gerry's driver, 'Big Eamon', and they embraced Helen and Seán.

I had compiled many obituaries for Volunteers killed in action during my years at *An Phoblacht*, looked at heartbreakingly young faces in treasured family photographs. Joe too was so young and I'd known him and the family personally. My abiding memory of him, the picture of him that will always be in my mind, is that of the last time I saw him. It was August, the summer before. Brendan and I were down for a few days. Joe came walking towards me, his hair glinting, golden in the sun. He was wearing a pair of dungarees and his hair was curling around his neck. He looked like a student, the world at his feet, his future before him, and of course that is what he was: a young man looking to the future. The fact was that he had chosen to pursue the cause of his country's freedom ahead of his own ambitions or desires. He and all the others who made that decision made a new future possible. It takes a special type of commitment for young people from the South to become involved in armed struggle without ever having directly experienced the provocation and motivating factor of British Army repression and state violence. To risk your freedom and your life in Joe's circumstances required great conviction and great courage. It also meant going against the huge weight of the anti-republican culture of the Irish Establishment, endless editorial tirades and denunciations from the pulpit, all aimed at defeating the IRA, and undermining reunification and independence. It meant swimming against an almost impossible tide. And yet young people did so—and Joe was one of them.

After mass, the cortege emerged from the church and I carried Joe's coffin opposite Helen as he was laid to rest in Sligo Cemetery.

It was heartbreaking.

As party president Gerry had authority to explore all forms of dialogue. In 1986 he privately met with John Hume, leader of the SDLP, and two years later this led to Sinn Féin and SDLP delegations meeting around the issue of the conflict and what would be required to resolve it. Whilst those talks foundered Gerry remained in contact with Hume and this led to the Hume/Adams' proposals. In November 1990 the British Secretary of State, Peter Brooke, made a speech, which was generally taken as being of significance, when he said that 'the British Government has no selfish strategic or economic interest in Northern Ireland.'

The background to the peace process has been exhaustively documented so there is no need to go over it all again, except for some recollections.

There were many, particularly in the Southern establishment, who opposed dialogue or who wanted to attach conditions on republicans to make engagement heavily onerous or smacking of humiliation and defeat. Peace is not just about the absence of conflict but about addressing the ultimate causes of conflict. There was also a section of British Intelligence who in a delusional way felt that military victory was still possible if only they were allowed to plough on. Their problem was that they had been repeatedly and confidently promising victory over the IRA yet the IRA campaign continued and its cumulative effect, especially its campaign in Britain, was forcing Britain to adopt a new approach. Many leading British military figures had publicly stated that there was a military stalemate. One, Brigadier James Glover, argued that the IRA could never be defeated militarily and would fight on until there was a political solution. However, others, particularly those in British Intelligence and the RUC Special Branch, pursued their dirty war through their loyalist surrogates whom they had rearmed and were directing.

One major report into collusion was by the former head of the London Metropolitan Police, John Stevens. He later said that out of 210 loyalists he had questioned, 207 turned out to be registered agents or informants for the British state. The malign hand of British Intelligence manipulating the situation in British interests, whether through using loyalists or dissident republicans, using compromised or amenable journalists to spread disinformation and undermine political leaders or republican morale, and using compromised or willing politicians, will be here until the *very* end. This is not a fantastical scenario or a conspiracy theory but is about the invisible powers behind framing public opinion because the prize of freedom and independence is so great—and so threatening to the establishment.

In early January 1994 the offices of *AP/RN* at 58 Parnell Square and head office at 44, where I worked, received two parcels wrapped in Christmas paper which had been posted in Dublin in December and one of which was addressed to me, including a threatening letter. Later, loyalists again threatened myself and Martin Mansergh who had been a long-standing advisor on the North to Fianna Fáil leaders, especially when Bertie Ahern was Taoiseach.

Suspicions were aroused and both parcels were removed to the carparks at the back. One exploded; the other partially exploded when being examined by the Irish Army who had removed the device to Cathal Brugha Barracks. It injured two bomb disposal experts. This was one week after another attack in Belfast against Sinn Féin Councillor Alex Maskey and his family. One of the worst killings in that period was a killing just three weeks before the IRA ceasefire. Kathleen O'Hagan from Creggan in County Tyrone was seven months pregnant when loyalists broke into her home and killed her in front of her children, the eldest of whom was just eight years of age.

At the 1992 Ard Fheis Sinn Féin released its latest discussion document, *Towards a Lasting Peace*, which was a follow-up to the earlier *Scenario for Peace* (1987). A lot of thought and debate was taking place publicly and privately. Meanwhile, the demonisation of the party continued afoot, especially in the South where we were banned from holding our conference in Dublin's Mansion House. In actual fact, the Mansion House had become too small a venue for us. We held conferences in Tallaght, in Ballyfermot, and another, a big one in Dundalk which was attended by the President of the Dominican Republic. Later, we would use the RDS—which I hated because of the Royal title in its name but it turned out to be a good venue and was where we would eventually hold our debate on policing in the North.

Jim Gibney's 1992 Bodenstown speech was brilliant, I thought. But he said it too soon. He referred to an internal Sinn Féin education seminar in Derry that had been addressed by a member of the Protestant community who said that republican appeals to unionists couldn't he heard above 'the deadly sound of gunfire', and, because of censorship and distortion, that was almost exclusively how our Movement was perceived. And the question Jim asked had profound implications:

'Does this reality mean that republicans are trapped inside a complex web of struggle from which they can't or don't emerge; hostages to an immediate past because of all the pain, suffering and commitment; to past views expressed, trenchantly, which in time solidified into unyielding principles? Does this reality mean that republicans are incapable of recognising that there is a different world to the one that existed in the mid-1960s or that they ignore the more recent changes sweeping across the globe? The answers to such questions cannot be found in the monosyllabic response, "No".'

Jim was signalling the need for negotiations but also for republicans to begin thinking laterally, imaginatively. It was a sobering remark. it was interpreted as 'we have to stop fighting' to reach other people. Which is true. It was powerful throughout, a careful and beautifully-worded speech. But the only thing that people heard and the media amplified was the phrase about the sound of our gunfire. People saw that as bringing an end to the armed struggle. Martin McGuinness's Bodenstown speech the year after Jim's address advanced that strategy a little bit further.

In politics (or around negotiations) there are statements made subtly or explicitly and they can represent an incremental shift in approach. Peter Brook's 1990 statement, and admissions by British military figures about a stalemate, fit into that category. As did Jim and Martin's. Martin emphasised that the Sinn Féin peace strategy was now a central part of our function as a political party. As Irish republicans our task is not to see the political difficulties through nationalist eyes alone but to also consider genuine unionist fears. He said:

'Our message to Protestants and unionists is a simple one. We want to live in peace with you. We realise that to achieve national reconciliation, the deep fears held by people must be addressed. We need to address those fears honestly and we accept that interim arrangements to allay understandable concerns may be required to facilitate the establishment of a dynamic Irish democracy that we could all be proud of. In an Irish national democracy those of the unionist tradition would command far greater political influence than they do now in union with Britain.'

In all the later congratulations and awards given to a variety of political personalities, up there on the international stage, in Oslo, in the spotlight, crowned on the front pages of magazines and newspapers, the fact remains that there would have been no Good Friday Agreement, no negotiations or cross-party talks, no ceasefires, without the influence of Gerry Adams who was the real instigator of the peace process. It is a tribute to his leadership, skill and powers of persuasion that he and Martin McGuinness brought the vast majority of republican activists, former prisoners and the IRA leadership on this path towards a lasting peace.

I was involved with the committee dealing with the Irish Government. Albert Reynolds was Taoiseach and wanted it to work; yes, on his terms, but he wanted it to work. Albert knew of course that there were secret contacts between the British and the Movement, and he would be receiving regular reports also about the exchanges between his officials and ourselves. He got on well with John Major but Major could not deliver on his promise of inclusive talks as he was in hock to the UUP. After the ceasefire was called in August 1994 the leader of the UUP, James Molyneaux, in an inadvertent and unguarded remark on radio, described the ceasefire as 'the greatest threat to the union' in fifty years.

Albert once told me that he told Major there was going to be a ceasefire. Major replied, 'Our intelligence services are telling me that there is no possibility of a ceasefire.' Albert replied: 'I always thought that IRA intelligence was always superior to your own!'

It was obvious that there were people who wanted the peace process to work, for a variety of reasons, and there were others who were determined that they weren't going to let it work because they knew that the end of conflict meant the end of imprisoning republicans, meant an end to censorship, meant amnesty and meant Sinn Féin emerging as an unencumbered political force.

One of the good things that Sinn Féin did consistently was to keep its base informed more than any other party or organisation did for its members. But you also had to be careful, of course, because the peace process had lots of enemies who didn't want it to work and would use distortion, rumours and lies to cause dissent or undermine the message. I remember a number of journalists, who would have been perceived as on the left or pro-republican, but who went beyond reporting and into consorting. They were truly exposed by their almost gleeful and exaggerated claims that large numbers of republicans in Tyrone and South Armagh had resigned, putting Adams and McGuinness in jeopardy. It was as if *their* struggle was being sold out! But they would never be going to jail or risking their lives. They lived off another man and woman's wounds.

Throughout this period there was no let-up by the Special Branch in the South against republicans. It was as if the prospect of peace enraged them also and they foresaw the source of their bounty evaporating. House raids continued and any visitors to our house were stopped and questioned. I had a coalman who delivered coal on a Friday. Even he was arrested and questioned. There were the odd light moments. Brendan and I and John McGuffin, the author/activist, were being followed and were stopped by the Branch at the side of the house.

'What's your name, Rita, and your address?' one asked. They all knew us. We were standing outside our own house. Our dog came running up to greet us.

'What's the dog's name?' asked a young Branch woman.

'Why?' I asked. 'Do you think he is a member of the Animal Liberation Front!'

McGuffin wrote up a story about it for his column in *An Phoblacht*, and after it appeared everyone would 'bark' at the local members of the Branch—who actually took it in good humour.

The peace process and the ceasefire led to the 'break out' of Sinn Féin—and our base and our enemies understood that. Our opponents weren't going to be able to keep us where they wanted us any longer. The guards, the politicians, the civil servants, the media, had done everything to corner us and demean and demonise us but had utterly failed.

In January 1994 the then minister in charge of the media, and future Irish President, Michael D. Higgins lifted Section 31 of the

Broadcasting Ban on Sinn Féin. However, RTÉ, precious as always, decided it would wait a week before interviewing Gerry Adams. I was having none of it. I organised Gerry to go on 98FM to be interviewed by Conor Lenihan (son of Fianna Fáil's Brian Lenihan). When Mick Nolan was bringing Gerry to the station Gerry said, 'Why am I going to 98FM?' and Mick replied, 'Because Rita O'Hare said you have to!'

Austin Currie, who began his early political life campaigning to end political discrimination, spoke out against the ending of Section 31, no doubt regretting the end of its discrimination against the legitimate voice of Irish republicanism.

It was also in early 1994 that US President Bill Clinton—against the advice of his own State Department and pressure from John Major—granted Gerry a visa to speak in the US.

So things were beginning to move but there would be great resistance to allowing Sinn Féin to join all-party talks. Britain and the unionists were given great succour when John Bruton took over as Taoiseach following the collapse of Albert Reynolds' government in November 1994 and supported and sympathised with unionist and British intransigence.

The peace process was beginning to lay bare the real cause of the conflict. The British lifted their own broadcasting restrictions against Sinn Féin in September 1994, a month into the ceasefire.

But many of those who wanted an end to conflict and saw the necessity of reform did not want republicans involved.

In my dealings with Irish governments and their many officials I met an elitist attitude on two fronts. They could be friendly and affable—until you presented the alternative, republican way of analysing the situation using a historic perspective. They didn't have the same appreciation as we did of the imperialist mindset of the Brits. None of the politicians in the South had lived under British rule. Yes, they dealt with them diplomatically and in international fora but their approach was never from an assertive national position but always from a pliant Twenty-Six-County perspective, anxious not to rock the boat or make things too difficult for London. Or for themselves.

Irish government figures and their officials literally looked down their noses at us and were of the opinion that we were incapable of negotiating, either at national or international level, that we were incapable of entering what's called mainstream politics, and that we would never proliferate as a political party and produce competent candidates. This was their *complacency* stage! Republicans in the North also experienced this attitude from the SDLP who thought it was their entitlement to lead the nationalist community. Of course, they all got their eyes opened and that is when *panic* set in and the entire Irish Establishment was more or less mobilised against 'the barbarians at the gate'!

To jump forward for a moment, Eoin Ó Broin hit a raw nerve in 2022 when he bluntly called for the chief economist in the Department of Finance to be sacked. The reaction against his remarks, the relentless pile-on, was instructive about the magnitude of the opposition to radical solutions to deal with the never-ending scandal of housing and homelessness. But it also showed just how powerful, influential and consolidated in office are senior civil servants.

What had happened was that a report by the Economic and Social Research Institute (ESRI) said that the state had the capacity to provide extra funding to build thousands of additional social homes and could manage it by borrowing €7bn a year. The report was rejected, indeed rubbished, by the senior civil servant with responsibility for the economic policy division in the Department of Finance. Ó Broin was speaking at a festival event when he made the remarks which sparked a backlash. While he retracted his original remark, he said he had spoken out of frustration and that the civil servant concerned should not continue to inform the government's housing policy.

There is no doubt that senior civil servants, regardless of elections, remain in power almost in perpetuity. Fianna Fáil and Fine Gael's values would be largely indistinguishable from their unelected advisors. Generally, the media establishment is in tune with this political culture even though commentators, puffed up by a sense of their own importance, criticise most of the parties—but always within the parameters of safe limits, even if there is the occasional call for a sacrificial head over some scandal. These powerful, vested interests— the establishment—rail against and prevent *meaningful* change: a shift of wealth and resources from the rich to the poor. Scratch the surface and what you have are class politics in operation.

The huge mistake our opponents made was assuming that we were incapable but also that we would be co-opted into their system.

It is often easy to exaggerate but the photo of Gerry Adams, alongside John Hume and Taoiseach Albert Reynolds outside government buildings in September 1994, shortly after the announcement of the IRA ceasefire, was powerful and iconic. For the first time since partition the leaders of Irish nationalism stood together, committed to peace and progress, two of them ostensibly committed to the Republican Movement's objective of reunification.

To maintain momentum, against the background of unionist resistance and John Major's laggard approach to the offer of peace, Albert Reynolds established the Forum for Peace and Reconciliation to which all parties were invited. Britain, the unionist parties and the loyalists boycotted it, but not the Alliance Party. The Forum met until early 1996 and received many submissions and commissioned a number of reports. It first met in Dublin Castle in October 1994. I remember Dick Spring, leader of the Labour Party, literally flattening himself against the wall when a Shinner walked past. I told him to catch himself on—and he did. I wasn't a formal delegate. Our party was represented by Gerry Adams, Pat Doherty and Lucilita Bhreatnach.

Every time I walked through the yard of Dublin Castle I thought of the Union Jack being hauled down there and replaced with the Tricolour and I was reminded of the lie that had condemned northern nationalists to second-class citizenship—the lie that the Treaty and the establishment of the Free State in 1922 represented 'the freedom to achieve freedom.'

Ironically, I managed to get on with Seamus Mallon in the Forum, despite his anti-republicanism. One thing about him was that he was clever. Secondly, in contrast to Hume, who held his cards close to this chest, Mallon was a party man. He was fiercely proud of the SDLP.

The Forum was well-resourced with generous and free lunches and dinners which I thought a total waste of money, disgraceful really. I am not sure whether the government thought it would impress us, that somehow we'd be bought over with Pavlova. However, we got on really well with the staff, the waitresses and the porters. We didn't treat them as if they didn't exist.

I used to go and talk to Albert Reynolds quite a lot, outside of the Forum sessions. I believed his intentions were good and when his government fell in November 1994 in came the disaster that was John Bruton, siding with Tory Prime Minister John Major. Albert wanted the Forum to work. Within Fianna Fáil he would have been considered to be on the 'republican' wing, though all these things are relative. He was not a 'college boy', not a Blackrock student, and was a self-made successful businessman before being elected for Longford-Westmeath in the mid-1970s. When I hear some people being lauded as these architects of the peace process, Albert Reynolds never got the kudos that he should have got.

The June general election in 1997 saw the election of Reynolds's successor, Bertie Ahern, just a month after Tony Blair became Labour Prime Minister in Britain.

This resetting of the peace process, their fresh and vigorous approach, resulted in the IRA renewing its ceasefire.

Rita (top right) on the steps of Government Buildings, September 1994. Mary Holland (middle, top left) with hands on hip. Courtesy: Rolling News

CHAPTER TEN

TO SOUTH AFRICA

Despite still being on the Wanted List and risking arrest and imprisonment by British authorities if I left the jurisdiction of the South, I ended up being Sinn Féin's representative in Washington for over twenty years. Before that I had twice travelled to South Africa and met Nelson Mandela.

There had been clandestine contacts between the African National Council (ANC) and the IRA during the armed struggle against white rule. Kader Asmal, a South African exile in Ireland, who founded the Irish Anti-Apartheid Movement and later became an ANC cabinet member, wrote in his memoir that the IRA had trained members of the ANC's armed wing Umkhonto weSizwe which had been led by Joe Slovo.

WORLD NEWS

Sth Africa facing new level of sabotage

JOHANNESBURG, Tuesday. — The spectacular bomb attack on South Africa's vital petroleum industry marks a new stage in black guerilla warfare in the country and is part of a co-ordinated plan by the African National Congress, according to the national intelligence chief, Dr Niel Barnard.

The Sunday night attack on the Sasol I oil-from-coal plant and a refinery at Sasolburg in the Orange Free State turned giant storage tanks into infernos and cost the country an estimated $7 million.

Mr Le Grange said last night that the exiled white South African Joe Slovo, who fled from the country in 1962, was now in Mozambique where he was co-ordinating ANC guerilla operations.

Asmal said the IRA carried out the reconnaissance for a major bomb attack on the Sasolburg oil refinery near Johannesburg in 1980 which had a devastating effect on the morale of the apartheid regime. Siobhán O'Hanlon was responsible for our South African desk. Siobhán had been arrested in Belfast in 1983 and sentenced, along with her co-accused the late Marie Wright, to seven years. Ironically, after her release, Marie, in 1989, was again arrested, this time with Pat, and both were sentenced to twenty-four years, but were part of the general release of political prisoners under the Good Friday Agreement. When Siobhán got out of prison she worked in the Belfast Republican Press Centre for a time before becoming Gerry Adams's secretary and was present at most of the Downing Street meetings. She was also a founding member of Féile an Phobail, the West Belfast festival.

In 2001, on the twentieth anniversary of the hunger strikes she, Pat, Cormac and Richard McAuley were on Robben Island when Gerry Adams unveiled a memorial to the hunger strikers in the prison yard where Mandela exercised during his long years in jail.

I just want to stop and say a few words about my friend Siobhán. She and her future husband Pat Sheehan were very good to me. Like me, she didn't suffer fools gladly and would call out phoneys. When Siobhán was dying she made a note to our mutual friend Trisha Ziff who had travelled from Mexico to say goodbye.

'Think of me now and again,' she wrote, in shaky handwriting. I think about her often. In October 2002 she had been diagnosed with breast cancer and died in 2006. She was only forty-three. Her and Pat's son Cormac was then just six. She was a great loss to the republican struggle and to me a great personal loss—someone I could call and talk to regularly.

In June 1995, as National Director of Publicity, I was on the first Sinn Féin delegation to meet with the ANC and Nelson Mandela who one year earlier had just become President of South Africa. There had been no express understanding sought from the Brits regarding my travel status. They could have attempted to serve an extradition warrant on me but how would that have looked? I flew out separately from the rest, travelling Dublin to Zurich, where I stayed a night. Gerry Adams, Richard McAuley and Chrissie McAuley flew via London. We were met at the airport by members of the ANC, including former death row prisoner Robert McBride.

South Africa, June 1995. With Martin McGuinness, Nelson Mandela, Gerry Kelly and Siobhan O'Hanlon

Our purpose was to learn from their experience of negotiating, as well as openly demonstrating solidarity between our two struggles. It was uplifting, humbling, inspiring. From the bantering and slegging, it was uncanny how similar was our and their humour. Humour, that great release common to us all in struggle, was very evident. The ANC chair, when introducing us, said, 'Comrade Gerry is here to represent Sinn Féin … And Comrade Rita is here to represent the IRA!'

At all our meetings what stood out for me was the prominence of women at all levels of the organisation.

Walter Sisulu's secretary, Rice Hodgson, embraced us and then in walked Walter who embraced Gerry. It was very emotional. He recalled being in prison in 1981 when the ANC closely followed the progress of Bobby Sands' hunger strike. (Later, in Durban, another activist, Sam Prahash, showed us where police fired on a solidarity march when Bobby Sands died. Subsequently, 'Sands' became the code word in smuggled prison letters about proposed hunger strikes.)

Rice remarked wryly that their prisoners, like ours, had once been called 'terrorists'. I had a particular empathy with Themba, a former political prisoner, who had served five years in jail, away from her children.

At the grave of Joe Slovo

Our ANC hosts also brought us to the Rugby World Cup semi-final in Durban where South Africa defeated France. South Africa later won the World Cup Final defeating the New Zealand All-Blacks. This was the tournament when Mandela supported the Springboks as a way of uniting the communities. The Springboks had been associated with the apartheid regime for decades. The story was later told in the film, *Invictus.*

Cape Town was lush and elegant with its colonial architecture and palm trees in comparison to Johannesburg. Our guide from the ANC's International Affairs Department, Emmanuel Nkuna, who brought us to the parliament, pointed out that not long ago he would not even have been allowed to walk on this street, never mind enter the building. We attended meetings all day in the parliament where Gerry did a Q & A before the Foreign Affairs Select Committee.

It was fascinating also to meet—given the hard choices facing unionism—General Constand Viljoen, formerly chief of the South African Defence Forces, a leader of the Afrikaner Freedom Front, a man who had upheld the old, apartheid regime, but who had now recognised and come to terms with democratic change and had opted for a negotiated settlement instead of a race war.

Everywhere we were warmly greeted. Chrissie and I got on exceptionally well with Adelaide Tambo, widow of former ANC President Oliver Tambo who had died in 1993 as change was rapidly taking place.

Back in Johannesburg we visited the townships of Soweto and Alexandra and the Phola Park squatter camp. At the community centre in Soweto we received a tremendous reception from the people and ANC representatives. We went by motorcade to Avalon Cemetery where we were met at the gates by members of the Veterans League and Women's League. People were carrying ANC flags and banners. The crowd was chanting, 'Viva the ANC, Viva! Viva Sinn Féin, Viva! Long live IRA, long live! Viva Joe Slovo, Viva!'

We proceeded to the grave of Joe Slovo, who as well as being the commander of Umkhonto weSizwe's armed campaign had also been leader of the South African Communist Party which he had joined in his teens. Joe had died of cancer at the age of sixty-eight, six months earlier. It was an intensely moving occasion. The singing, the chanting, the colours of the flags, the speeches, the way we were welcomed is something I shall never forget.

Joe is buried among the people he fought for all his life. His is a simple grave. No mausoleum could have served his memory better. When the crowd sang the national anthem, 'Nkosi Sikelel' iAfrika', their spirit and dignity was evident in every note. We were all deeply affected. We then went to Phola Park.

Robert McBride explained the social and economic challenges the new government faced. In the township and in this squatter camp lived three-and-a-half-million people, most of them with only basic amenities, the stark legacy of apartheid. The ANC was pledged to devoting massive resources in building, health and education programmes.

A big crowd was waiting for us about a mile from the camp. Again, women were much in evidence with banners and flags, singing a welcome to us. There was also a 'band of warriors' from the camp, there to 'guard' Gerry. I walked towards them but was held back by Emanuel who told me not to go too near or touch any of them because when they gather as warriors they do not talk to or engage with anyone outside their own circle.

We walked, danced and sang on the way to the camp. People joined in, dancing the Toyi-toyi which had been defiantly used in confrontations with the South African police. Feet stomped to a particular rhythm, accompanied by chanting. The women took us by the hand and explained what the songs and slogans they were chanting meant. Even I, who can't dance, joined in. There were children everywhere. Gerry joked that it was like being back in Springhill! A tiny child, a boy about three years old, danced and sang, leading the way to a reception in the middle of the camp where we were welcomed in the speeches. The spirit and dignity of the people was deeply affecting. But we couldn't stay long because there was another reception committee waiting for us in Alexandra township.

No film or photograph could prepare you for the reality of the deprivation. Yet there were schools, a community centre and a health centre, and an ANC office where the staff had ambitious plans for the future. Driving through the camp, which had also been raided by death squads and suffered many killings, I found myself crying and was also thinking about the people of Springhill being murdered by British soldiers. It was Sunday and despite the unbelievable conditions the lanes were full of people, beautifully dressed and making their way to church. A girl of about fifteen stepped out of a hut. Her hair was braided, she wore a gleaming white T-shirt, Levi jeans and Doc Marten boots like any teenager in Ireland. My tears were of admiration for the spirit that could endure, resist and rise above the injustice and cruelty of the regime that had created these conditions. They were also tears of anger that this had gone on for so long. Jerome comforted me and said, 'Be strong.' I found it hard to sleep that night, to escape the images of that day, before the *big* day and meeting Nelson Mandela.

Monday began with a series of meetings with the ANC leadership, the people who had been centrally involved in the negotiations. Our first was with Cyril Ramaphosa, ANC General Secretary. Gerry presented him with a Long Kesh harp. He was very interested in the names of the prisoners who had signed the base of the artefact, along with their prison sentences ranging from 20, 25 to 30 years, similar to those handed down to ANC members in the past.

Then came the meeting with Mandela.

All that had been written and said about him could not capture the actual magnitude of his dignity and bearing, the sparkle and vigour in his eyes. He was warm, kind and humorous. The British Government had lobbied hard against him meeting us. Similarly, he had been heavily criticised by the British (who were then secretly talking to republicans) when on his first visit to Ireland in 1992 he called upon the British Government to begin talks with Irish republicans. Also at the meeting were Kader Asmal and Walter Sisulu.

Mandela called me his 'little warrior' and said I was to stand in front of him.

We travelled up to Pretoria where we met Deputy President Thabo Mbeiki in his office at parliament buildings and, later, Roelf Meyer of the National Party. It was Meyer, along with Cyril Ramaphosa who brokered the constitutional breakthrough in 1993 at a time when it seemed that South Africa's only future was civil war. Meyer said, 'We not only understood each other but we trusted each other. We told each other the truth.'

On our last day we were received at the headquarters of the South African Communist Party by Charles Ngakula, General Secretary; Deputy General Secretary Jeremy Cronin and Helena Doiny. Helena, Joe Slovo's widow, was presented with a Celtic Cross made by republican prisoners, and a presentation for Chris Hani's family was accepted by Charles. The assassination of Chris Hani by a right-wing Akrikaner group in Johannesburg in 1993 was aimed at derailing the peace process and provoking civil war. The circumstances of his killing was a lesson we took on board, the need to be extra vigilant, especially in the run-up to negotiations and thereafter. Chris had been an eloquent, inspirational and charismatic leader of both Umkhonto we Sizwe and the South African Communist Party.

Over lunch, Gerry gave an assessment of the peace process. We learnt a great deal. The spirit of forbearance and forgiveness from a people who had been so cruelly treated was one thing that particularly struck me.

I went back to South Africa two years later—and again there was no guarantee sought from or given by the Brits regarding a threat of my extradition. On this occasion we were attending an all-party conference in the Western Cape as guests of the ANC and the National Party. Ironically, it was titled the 'gathering of the minds'. It was hoped that being several thousand miles from home and away from the prying eyes of the media, that ourselves and the unionists would feel much freer to talk and exchange ideas.

However, the unionists made it clear from the start that they would be having no contact with Sinn Féin. Ulster Unionist Party leader David Trimble and Democratic Unionist Party deputy leader Peter Robinson sought guarantees they would be 'hermetically sealed off' from us: us being myself, Siobhán O'Hanlon, Gerry Kelly and our chief negotiator Martin McGuinness.

Robinson told the *Irish Times*: 'We need to know that we will travel separately, lodge separately, socialise separately, meet people separately—apartheid in fact.' Their decision amazed the ANC whose role was to explain how they had successfully worked with their South African counterparts to reach a settlement. Nelson Mandela had to make two farewell speeches—one for Sinn Féin, one for the others. The unionists appeared to have no conception of how petty they appeared on the world stage.

Editor's note

Rita was Sinn Féin's representative to North America from 1998 to 2020. Due to visa restrictions, she was unable to travel to Canada but remained in constant contact with Friends of Sinn Féin in Canada.

During her time in Washington she worked with numerous members of Congress and the administrations of four presidents: Clinton, Bush, Obama, and Trump. In 2004 she also met with President Jimmy Carter.

She represented Sinn Féin through the many twists and turns of the peace process from the signing of the Good Friday Agreement, attacks by dissident republicans, disbandment of the RUC, demilitarisation, the putting beyond use of arms by the IRA, the election of Martin McGuinness as deputy First Minister, the establishment of the Police Service (NI), Sinn Féin moving to support the new policing arrangements, the introduction of Brexit and the rise of Sinn Féin as the largest political party in Ireland.

Throughout her tenure in the US there were many challenges as the British Government and at times the Irish Government sought to sideline Sinn Féin. But she would not be silenced.

Her reach was not confined to DC. She was on first-name terms with state representatives and councillors, and labour and Irish American leaders across the US. Pick a point in the map and Rita knew someone there or knew someone who knew someone. One newspaper wrote: 'The redhead who woos corporate America ... and puts up more mileage than an astronaut.'

She was a constant in a changing world, making her way to check up on friends as soon as she could, following 9/11.

For many years Rita was the sole point at which Sinn Féin and US foreign policy met.

Through all these challenges she built relationships and remained a ferocious advocate for peace, political progress, and Irish unity.

She gained the respect and trust of many. A one-woman, diplomatic—and at times undiplomatic—force of nature.

CHAPTER ELEVEN

TO AMERICA

I had not been involved at all with the USA or the Connolly House group within the party which worked on bringing North America into the peace process and bringing Irish republicans into North America. Back in 1993 a number of Irish-American businessmen and politicians met with Gerry Adams in the party's West Belfast headquarters, Connolly House. Among them were Bill Flynn, Chuck Feeney, Congressman Bruce Morrison and Niall O'Dowd, and they were nicknamed, the Connolly House Group. They provided great impetus and I think successive Irish governments resented their independence, that they weren't a pawn of theirs, and government had to respond to the fresh momentum they brought to resolving the political deadlock. Bill and Bruce were two of the hardest-working people on the question of Ireland.

I was involved in a small way over the successful attempts to secure the visa for Gerry to get into the States in early 1994. We all knew that it would be a big thing if he got in.

The August 1994 ceasefire, a few months later, would open up all sorts of opportunities and potential. The US's lifting of the ban on veteran IRA leader Joe Cahill on the eve of the ceasefire was also of major significance. Jean Kennedy-Smith, whom Bill Clinton had appointed as US Ambassador to Ireland in 1993, was the ideal pick and hugely influential in the decision around Joe, and many other decisions. Jean lobbied Nancy Soderberg of the National Security Council and Clinton then spoke to Albert Reynolds, for reassurances I think. Although Jean retired as ambassador in July 1998 her contribution cannot be overstated.

My role had been in briefing her on the peace process and we had really warmed to each other. When I had my first cancer diagnosis in 1996 and had a mastectomy in the Mater Hospital Jean sent books to me. We had similar temperaments, being impatient with negative people. We got along extremely well. Indeed, after I took up my role in America I was at her daughter Amanda's wedding in Bridgehampton, and was driven there by my friend Larry Downes, a New York lawyer and a great Irish republican. Larry still jokes about having been my chauffeur and waiting with the other chauffeurs for four hours and me not even throwing him a shrimp. I remember Larry's sister Moira asking me was I not star-struck and I replied: 'They are who they are as long as they are President or Senator. I'm who I am all the time.'

Moira was another one of those people never acknowledged: a great supporter of the peace process, and very generous. She offered me use of the cottage for a holiday but with my strict and limited routine I had to decline. That evening, after the wedding, Larry and I shared a drink with Bill Barry, the famous FBI agent and friend of Bobby Kennedy, who was a strong supporter of the peace process.

Jean was alert, focused, dedicated, charming and intelligent. She was thoughtful and calm, even during subsequent crises and would never panic or allow frustration to dictate her response. I remember the night a few years later when the IRA ended its ceasefire with the bombing of Canary Wharf in London. I went to the US ambassador's residence in Phoenix Park to break the news. A very pale John Hume was already there, sitting in an armchair with a drink and a cigarette, totally shattered, despondent. Jean went over and patted him on the leg and assured him that it would be okay, the peace could be put back together. And she was right.

(I remember the following morning I came out of my home to find RTÉ journalist Charlie Bird standing shivering in the garden. He'd been waiting for hours hoping to get some exclusive but instead he got brought into the kitchen for a cup of coffee. He was one journalist that I could get on really well with, and I also got to know his family.)

Jean was highly-attuned to the complexities of presidential power and politics and so she critically understood where there would be resistance and where there would be accommodation. She totally *got* it, the importance of the peace process and how Clinton's involvement could change and facilitate the situation. She also knew it would be good for the US.

She understood personal suffering, having had two brothers assassinated, John and Bobby, and in fact she was at the event in the hotel in Los Angeles in June 1968 when Bobby was killed.

She loved being the ambassador and I think she was the best ambassador we ever had. I think she was often treated very unfairly by certain sections of the press because, firstly, she was a woman and secondly because she was a Kennedy. You often heard the snide remarks, which were basically sexist, aimed at diminishing her reputation and authority.

At the embassy I also got to know Ned Nolan, who was very helpful, and his wife Patricia. They were delighted to be in Ireland at this exciting time. I usually dealt with Ned in relation to visas for other people, not myself at this stage.

The British Government had strongly objected to Joe getting into the States, as had the US State Department. The Brits had always tried to keep Ireland below the international radar so that they could portray it as a domestic dispute, not an international problem. That was why it was essential for us that America become a player in the peace process. America could play a role that British and Irish governments could not or would not play because they had a vested interest. The American Government had less vested interest within the domestic politics of Ireland but we hoped that they would have a vested interest in having a foreign policy in Ireland that produced a successful peace process despite the worst excesses of the sectarian northern state. They have proved to have done exactly that.

Our plan was to make the American Government take on this important international role. We looked at other areas in the world, South Africa for instance, and we had seen how the ANC had successfully used international opinion to get rid of the apartheid regime. We looked and learned from other people.

Joe Cahill on his visit went to brief an important and huge constituency—our Irish-American supporters who had stood by the struggle through thick and thin and had often been demonised as deluded romantics. The ones who were really deluded were their critics who had no idea of how important, committed and far-reaching into society were these first, second and third generation Irish. Their continued support and influence was crucial—and, indeed, flourished after the ceasefire and after the Good Friday Agreement.

My other, limited connection to America around this time was that I had got to know Ciarán Staunton. Ciarán was instrumental in establishing and directing the operations of the recently-established Friends of Sinn Féin (FOSF), set up post-ceasefire. FOSF was being run administratively from New York by Fay Devlin and Larry Downes and held its first fundraiser in March 1995, emceed by Fionnula Flanagan, the actress, who was brilliant. She became a dear friend and put her head about the parapet regardless of the flak, the lies and disinformation. She went on to host a huge event in Dublin in 2002 which was very important to the families of dead IRA Volunteers— *Tirghra* (Love of Country). It paid tribute to their courage and sacrifices. Fionnuala also endorsed Martin when he ran for the Irish presidency in 2011. And on another occasion she threw a big birthday party for Gerry at her and her husband Garrett's Beverly Hills home. There were many well-known actors at it and I sat talking to Harry Dean Stanton. Fionnula was born in Cabinteely, not far from where we live. An uncle of hers who was in the IRA was shot during the Tan War.

When Ciarán was here for meetings he would call into our press office. He was outgoing and very friendly. He knew Dawn Doyle, who a few years later would succeed me as Director of Publicity. Through Ciarán I met and struck up a great friendship with Niall O'Dowd, the Irish-American publisher and confidante of Bill Clinton. Niall and I get on great and slag each other with such abuse that sometimes people look on horrified! Niall published newspapers aimed at the diaspora and younger Irish-Americans. Ciarán actually met his future wife, Orlaith, Niall's sister, through Niall and through working on the peace process. Tragically, in 2012 their twelve-year-old son Rory died of undiagnosed and untreated sepsis. Ciarán and Orlaith then sent up the Rory Staunton Foundation for Sepsis Prevention and have been instrumental in campaigning globally for mandatory sepsis protocols which have saved thousands of lives. In 2022 Michael D. Higgins presented them with Ireland's Presidential Distinguished Service Award for the Irish Abroad.

In 1997 I received a message from Niall inviting me to take part in a panel discussion sponsored by the *Irish Voice* on the influence of the media in the peace process, and whether the media helped or hindered a resolution of the conflict. It was to be hosted by Jim Dwyer, a Pulitzer-Prize winning American journalist with the *New York Times* who had a track record exposing injustices.

Of course, my immediate answer was, 'Thanks, Niall. But I can't get into the States.'

He said: 'I wouldn't be so sure. Don't refuse on that basis.'

'I'm not refusing. I'm just telling you I can't imagine why I would get a visa.'

I mentioned the invitation to Jean Kennedy-Smith. I said there was no chance of me getting a visa and she said, 'You should try. You haven't got a refusal until you try.'

Next thing, Gerry rings me. 'If you get a visa would you go?' I said I would—never imagining for a second that I would get a visa. But I got the bloody visa! It allowed me to visit between 18 November and 17 December, 1997. My antenna wasn't as attuned then to the machinations that were going on behind my back! I was worried about my flight being diverted to Britain—in some actual emergency—or an extradition warrant being served on me in the US. Opinion was that if a visa was cleared in the States the Brits would not be so foolish to act and cause a political row. They hadn't made a move when my visits to South Africa were so public.

So, I went. The event was scheduled for the 20 November. My cousin Pat and Siobhán were there to greet me at the airport along with Ciarán Staunton. I think Gerry Kelly and Richard McAuley were already there. We went to Manhattan and had lunch. I stayed in Upper West Side in an apartment belonging to the sister of Pat's husband, Moses.

I loved how people in New York walked everywhere. I woke Pat up very early the next morning and demanded that we go walking. The weather was gorgeous and we walked from 86th and Riverside down Broadway to Columbus Circle and back up Central Park West.

I loved New York from the very minute I got there, the rush of it. I am a terribly impatient person. I am dreadfully impatient and I just loved that the city moved so fast and there was so little time for people to fiddle around.

We went to the event which was quite successful though not very big. I met a lawyer, a wonderful woman, called Mary Pike. In a hotel, the Southgate, owned by two Irish fellas, I met Kathleen Curtin from Listowel. We immediately hit it off. Her father was a Sinn Féin councillor back home. The following night we all went to the Irish Northern Aid Testimonial Dinner and were joined by Shannon Eaton, a long-time activist and very good friend. Shannon had looked after Gerry during his forty-eight-hour visit to New York in January 1994 and she was of great support to me in the USA. Anybody who knows me knows that I am not into fashion! I prefer jeans and sweatshirts. But Shannon took me in hand and made sure I had proper business attire for my countless meetings and suitable clothes for dinner and other events.

Pat and I then went down to Washington where I stayed with her and Moses. They lived in a modest, four-bedroomed house with their

143

three children, Molly, Daniel and Anna, in American University Park, in the north west of the city.

Relaxing with her cousin Pat at her home in Washington

My mother Maureen was the eldest of seven and had three sisters—Pat, Rita, and, my cousin Pat's mother, Kathleen who was the youngest. During the war Kathleen was a secretary for the British War Office in Belfast when her siblings Pat and Rita were working at hospitals in London. Kathleen had gone to visit them but while in England travel restrictions were imposed, stranding her in London, so she transferred to the British War Office there.

At the end of the war she worked in Germany on the refugee relief effort and it was in Frankfurt, in the American zone, where she met her soon-to-be husband, a Polish army officer, Richard Kolm, who had been a POW for over five years. After his release, he worked at the children's camp in Frankfurt for displaced persons. They married and moved to the US in 1948. Inspired by his work with POWs and displaced persons, Richard went on to become a sociologist and tenured professor at the Catholic University of America in Washington.

Kathleen and Richard had two boys and one girl, like Maureen and Billy. So Pat and I were like the sisters we never had.

Pat worked as a volunteer in the Sinn Féin office in the Dupont Centre, building up the donor base. The office was managed by Mairéad Keane from Dublin who had been in charge for several years but was due to step down. Mairead had come through the fall-out from the breakdown of the ceasefire, a hugely difficult time for her. But she held the office together. Pat was familiar with the ins and outs of Capitol Hill because she also worked as a grant-writer for the National Immigration Forum, a non-profit, pro-immigration advocacy group. Her organisation was concerned about her links to Sinn Féin because of the way Gerry and myself were depicted in the media but Pat was dedicated to her solidarity work.

The Dupont Office, which was quite expensive to rent, was sponsored by the Irish-American philanthropist Chuck Feeney and was aimed at establishing a Sinn Féin political presence to promote the peace process. It was in a modern commercial office building near Dupont Circle. Chuck had committed to financing the project for three years. I went to the office and met Mairéad. Among her staff was Colleen Lansdown, a fascinating young African-American woman working as a receptionist; Ciaran Clifford (who was thinking of moving to Ireland); and an intern called Greg O'Loughlin from upstate New York whose family were very republican (that is, pro-Irish republican). He was a university student but had volunteered to work in the office during the summer holidays. He had a great sense of humour and was diligent in his work. In 2003 Greg moved to Nashville to finish his teaching degree. At the time of writing he is FOSF's Director of Operations.

Chuck Feeney was a wonderful, humble man. He actually reminded me in a way of my father and my mother. They had absolutely no interest in material possessions. It just never entered their heads that this was what marked a person or what made a person. I met Chuck and I am glad I did. He touched everyone he was involved with. He was impressive, very unassuming, lacked all artifice, and was extremely generous. Quietly and without fanfare, Chuck also gave away more than $8 billion through The Atlantic Philanthropies, a private charitable foundation that he established and financed.

Chuck Feeney's name, reputation and integrity lent us an enormous amount of credibility. The fact that he would stick his neck out—he was absolutely confident about the peace process—improved our standing generally as well as becalmed people, given that some of us had been deeply involved in the war and this would unnerve many folk.

He was really clued in and would listen attentively to what you were saying. He certainly could analyse very quickly and was certainly not interested in listening to bullshit. Not that I ever talked bullshit! He could spot smarm and flattery a mile off.

He had a real dry sense of humour. The first time we met I hadn't needed glasses. But America ruined my eyesight! Anyway, I just used those glasses that you buy off the shelf in one of the convenience stores. I thought they were great. They were only a few dollars. We were out together and he gave me something to read. I cannot remember what it was, but I took out the glasses and put them on.

He looked at me and he said, 'Oh, you have the same optometrist as me. Duane Reade.' Duane Reade is a chain of cost-saving pharmacy and convenience stores. I laughed and said, 'Yes, if I lose them it doesn't matter. They only cost three dollars. All I need them for is magnification.'

Chuck even buys his watches over the counter at CVS. 'Why would you want anything else? It tells the time,' he said. He was quite basic in his requirements and used to laugh at Niall who would always have the latest in mobile technology. Chuck hated mobile phones. We were waiting on Niall one day in this little diner we used somewhere around Park Avenue and 50th: I can't remember its name. Niall arrived and shortly afterwards his mobile rang. Chuck pulled out a picture of a mobile, cut out of a magazine ad, and pretended to be talking into it!

Chuck is a hugely interesting man, too. But he does keep himself and his family very private, though I have met his wife several times.

I wasn't long back in Ireland from that first visit when Gerry rang to find out how I had got on. I said it was fascinating, particularly New York. I hadn't thought I would like the US but I loved the general attitude of Americans of going and getting something done as quickly as possible if it needs to be done. Saying that, was a mistake! Next day, Gerry rings again.

'You know Mairead's coming home,' he says.

'Yes. She mentioned that.'

'Will you do it?'

'Fucking no. No way.'

'What do you mean, "No"?'

'I know nothing about America. Absolutely nothing.'

'Well, will you think about it?'

All my publicity work, which kept me extremely busy, revolved around the peace process.

I said no to him three times. Then he phoned Brendan.

'It'll only be for two years,' he told Brendan. 'Two years and it'll not involve *all* the time. A month there. A month back here. We can be flexible.'

Brendan asked me if I actually wanted to take on the role and I repeated that I did not.

'I do not know the territory. I don't know the people.'

'But would you be interested in doing it?'

'I've actually not even though about that.'

The kids had all left home but France's son, Aodhán, our grandchild, lived with us. He was about fifteen and was preparing for the Leaving Cert. So, although I was reluctant, I was persuaded by it being time-limited and then someone else would take over the role. I also knew that Larry Downes would help me. And there were others such as Gerry Lally and Kathleen Curtin who would get me connections. Larry was superb about advising us on US law, right down to the small dos and don'ts. Our opponents were always on the alert, watching for any missteps and ready to make a big story out of whatever they could.

When Gerry announced that I would be replacing Mairéad a British Embassy spokesperson in Washington, before I applied for a working visa, responded by saying that an arrest warrant was outstanding and could only be lifted by a court order and action by Downing Street. The spokesperson said that Britain had still to decide whether it would seek my extradition. Other republicans had been able to get into America legally and carry out political work without impediment. Mairéad being an American citizen had all those things that would not restrict her from being there for a considerable length of time, or from going back and forth. Seán Mac Brádaigh, who became the party's Director of Publicity and editor of *An Phoblacht*, was also a US citizen, having been born in Connecticut in the late 1960s. Derry's Mitchell McLaughlin, who became Speaker at Stormont, also managed to get in. But most of our senior people had been in jail and accumulated often more than one or two sentences. However, once people had elected status it was slightly easier.

Because of my conviction over smuggling explosives into Portlaoise I also needed a waiver from the US Justice Department. We got over all hurdles but conditions were quite strict: the authorities required to know my every step, my itinerary, venues for meetings and where I was staying. I remember, later, I was at a function in the prestigious Union League Club of New York in Park Avenue, a private, conservative social club with a dress code etiquette and not my usual haunt, when a newly-appointed official from the British consul general's office, approached me, fairly amiably, and introduced himself. He noted, with a grin, that if I stayed beyond my thirty days it would be his responsibility to sign the extradition warrant. I wasn't fazed and we both laughed.

I felt that the US Government wouldn't give me a visa if they thought there was the slightest chance of London applying to extradite me while I was in New York or Washington and sparking a major row during an ongoing peace process, stranding me in the States and tying me up in a long legal process. Besides affecting me and my family personally, an extradition attempt by the Brits would be seen as an act of bad faith, would anger republicans, and be exploited by others less committed to peace as proof of British deceit. Even later, there was always the possibility of something fortuitous happening: some minor immigration official looking at a computer screen and ordering an arrest, followed by unionists and the right-wing press in Britain demanding the US return me to Belfast for trial. In 2016, Gerry, who had an *official* invitation, was refused entry by the US Secret Service to the annual St Patrick's Day reception in the White House. I was skeptical about the explanation they subsequently gave which was extremely weak. The Secret Service said they sent an email to their superior to see if they should let Gerry into the reception but their boss had gone for a jog because it was a nice day and didn't see the email until after Gerry had left. Back in 2005 I had been temporarily denied a visa over a very simple departure from protocol. In April I had notified the State Department that myself and Sinn Féin negotiator Gerry Kelly would be going to New York to meet Bill Flynn, a major supporter of the peace process and chair of Mutual of America. We learnt late in the day that Bill was in Florida—he was actually ill and unable to travel—and so we flew down there to meet him. What happened next was salutary. A few weeks later I was due to accompany Martin McGuinness to New York, and on to Washington to meet State Department officials. However, I was denied a visa—temporarily, as it turned out—because I went to Florida without seeking permission.

It was Bill Clinton who cleared my visa in the first place, otherwise I might not have got in. There were those in the government who were often not on the same page and some of those could try to stick a spanner in the works.

The damned visa would turn out to be a real pain. I had never any intention of staying in the US permanently. But having to apply every single time was a grind. In the beginning I was going to the States much more frequently than now to establish myself and get myself known, to build up a solid network, and to get a good sense of everything I needed to know. I was always very clear, very clear to myself from the beginning what my role was. It was about Sinn Féin, it was about Ireland, and it was about the peace process. That is what I did. Everything that I did was framed to support those things. I was not there to change America, except about Ireland.

I had to apply for a visa on every occasion, a temporary visa, then return to Dublin from where I could apply again. But there was never a glitch after the Florida incident. There were many people who helped me enormously with logistics, making political and personal connections and providing good sound solid advice on US politics and analysis. One of the best was Bill Flynn who was part of the Connolly House Group. I rarely travelled into New York without meeting Bill, as did Gerry. His insights into US, Irish Government and British Government politics was invaluable. British Secretaries of State, Irish Government Ministers, PSNI Chief Constables and others would regularly meet him and he was very forthright in his assessment of their motivations and actions.

When Jean Kennedy-Smith heard I was coming to DC as Sinn Féin's representative she rang her brother, Senator Ted Kennedy. So, when Mairead, who was leaving, organised a reception to introduce me, Ted Kennedy came along and brought two or three other senators.

On my second trip, around St Patrick's Day, 1998, we were being repeatedly asked about the negotiations. Gerry was speaking at the Tower View Ballroom in Queens and he laid down some markers that informed our approach to the talks. Until now, republicans had been excluded from all discussions around governance in Ireland. The British, the unionists, the Irish Government and the SDLP, after decades of failure, now had to accept that without our involvement there could be no meaningful or lasting solution. Gerry stated that we would not be involved in a settlement that does not address the release of the political prisoners, RUC members being given their redundancy notices, and that does not address the fundamental principles of equality and parity. The day before he had been in London meeting Tony Blair and he had told him, 'If we cannot have a united Ireland by May [the talks' deadline], then we cannot have a United Kingdom either,' meaning, as far as we were concerned, that the new dispensation was about uncoupling the North from the union with Britain and moving towards reunification.

One of the first trips I organised in my new role was in November 1998 when Gerry and I visited Mexico City at the invitation of my dear friend Trisha Ziff. He opened the exhibition 'Hidden Truths - Bloody Sunday' at the *Centro de la Imagen* (the Center for the Image). Californian Senator Tom Hayden and Tom Patchett, director of the Track 16 Gallery in Santa Monica, accompanied us on the trip.

Trisha curated the exhibition and had edited a companion book of essays, photos and images. Tony Doherty and Elaine Brotherton, relatives of two of the men killed on Bloody Sunday, who both worked on the exhibition, were introduced along with Don Mullan, author of *Eyewitness Bloody Sunday*. Tony was just nine when his father was shot dead for taking part in a civil rights march and Elaine was three when her uncle, William McKinney was killed by the Paras.

The following day, at Anahuac University, Gerry gave a lecture and afterwards the Academy of Mexican International Law conferred on him their Order of Law, Culture and Peace. Previous recipients of the award include two Secretary Generals of the United Nations and Polish Solidarity leader Lech Wałęsa. We next met with Foreign Affairs Minister Rosario Green and Under Secretary Juan Rebolledo and briefed them about the progress of the Irish peace process.

It was an extremely busy schedule and we also met with members of the Commission of Concord and Pacification of Chiapas (COCOPA); the Mayor of Mexico City, Cuauhtemoc Cardenas, Federal Deputies Gilberto Rivas and Carlos Zubieta. We also attended a private reception where we met leaders of opinion in arts, literature, politics and church figures.

Even though I would get to meet Presidents, Senators and Congress members, I was never in awe of anyone. I always made sure to get talking to waiters and waitresses, doormen, taxi drivers and workers about their lives and experiences which I often found fascinating. I also enjoyed the variety of people we met: trade unionists, writers, poets and actors. The peace process really liberated many people who were sympathetic to Irish republicanism and the cause of reunification but who could not chance being dubbed fellow-travellers of the IRA. Understandably, they simply would not have the arguments to explain the conflict or refute British propaganda with the same fervour and conviction as those of us who experienced the war at first hand.

There were also inspirational stories from people who had left Ireland, particularly the North, because in terms of work and prospering it was a wasteland for nationalists. Pat Donaghy from Carrickmore in

With Greg O'Loughlin, Larry Downes and
Gerry, July 2022

With Richard McAuley, Terry O'Sullivan, Gerry and Brian Donohue

Tyrone had emigrated at the age of eighteen in 1959 and had gone on to establish Structure Tone, one of the major and most successful construction businesses in New York. But he never forgot his roots and became a great supporter of ours and the peace process. Tragically, his sister Peggy's son was assassinated along with two other republicans in Cappagh in 1991. The rifle used to kill twenty-three-old John Quinn in 1991 was part of a shipment of weapons to loyalists facilitated by British Intelligence.

Solidarity with workers in USA

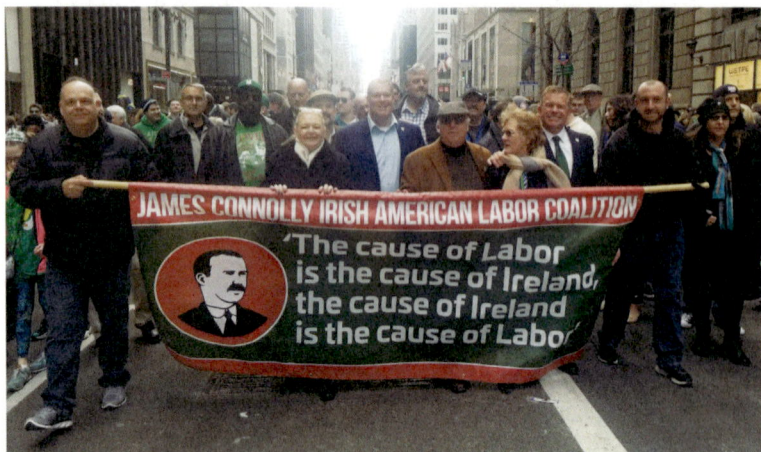

New York march, St Patrick's Day, 2018

Sustaining an office and staff in Washington is quite expensive. Both Pat and Larry Downes had been on the lookout for new office space when we had to leave Dupont. We rented the main floor of a lovely old Federal-style townhouse on Stanton Square on Capitol Hill from a retired, elderly couple who lived on one floor, we working on the other floor. But the important thing was to be on the Hill, up there briefing. Initially, our Capitol Hill office served as an information clearinghouse and a suitable location for the kind of 'meet-and-greet' receptions Washington is famous for. Whenever Gerry and Martin came to Washington, they and many other Sinn Féin delegates met with US politicians and donors at receptions hosted by Friends of Sinn Féin. Greg was very eager to learn more about computer technology and he was good at it so he did all that stuff. We'd receive the headlines and important stories from Ireland every morning thanks to a faxed news clipping service. Dozens of photocopied newspaper front pages and press releases would squawk through the fax machine every morning. I'd read them as they came off the machine, and highlight key phrases, underline the most relevant parts.

I always believed in being well-organised, especially when it came to our reps coming over. Every detail was thoroughly and meticulously planned; every minute of every visit was fully booked. From handling the flights, to who would collect and return them to the airport, where they would stay, where they would eat, the amount of free time they would have (and it was usually very limited), the train schedules, how they would get to venues (walk, car, train). I mean, every detail would be meticulously handled in advance of any visit. When a Sinn Féin representative/spokesperson stepped foot in the US they had nothing to think about or worry about while here, their entire itinerary was carefully planned. I made sure I knew the entrance/exits for the venues as well as the hotels. This was always done at least a week in advance and confirmed with everyone a day in advance. I was a bit obsessive in this regard!

My accommodation was straightforward: I stayed with Pat and Moses and also had 'office' facilities at their home so I could work at nights and make the most productive use of my time in the States. I didn't need a car in Washington as the transport system, the Metro, was so efficient, quick and reliable to Union Station and was only a fifteen-minute walk from my cousin's house. Pat and I were convinced her phone was bugged. So, when we had to discuss important business we would go for walks or sit on her front steps in the evening with a glass of whiskey. With a few drinks we might become boisterous—which neighbours in that area never did! I also had to curtail my language!

I avoided the Irish pubs like the plague. There was one called The Irish Times behind the Phoenix Park Hotel where Mairéad and visitors from Sinn Féin had stayed. It was owned by a nice man, Danny Coleman. On St Patrick's Day it was packed with Irish people and Irish politicians, Guinness and whiskey galore. Gerry was tormented there. You couldn't get a coffee or a quiet corner. Later, Joseph Smith, originally from Ardoyne, became a close and very good friend. When he opened his restaurant in DC we began receiving our visitors there, which was a saving, but more importantly it was a quieter and more relaxed venue. I received requests all the time for Gerry to come to pubs that had been opened and I always refused. I just said, 'I'm really sorry, but Gerry doesn't do that type of thing.' When Pat and Moses moved to Ireland in 2004 it was at Joe's that I stayed. Joseph also arranged hotels in DC and along with Todd Allen regularly travelled with Gerry by train and by plane as we travelled the USA.

It was Joseph who introduced me to Terry O'Sullivan of LiUNA (Laborer's International Union of North America) which opened up a whole new front for us in the States with the trade unions and its Irish-American members. Terry, in turn, was to introduce me to dozens of others, representatives like Jim O'Callaghan, head of the Pipefitters Union, and even union people in, say, San Francisco. We went to Los Angeles and other places where there are good strong unions, including the Screen Actors Guild. You met movie stars, some of whom would come to our functions. Talk about falling on your cushioned feet when I met Terry!

The unions were experts at networking. They were so generous about opening doors for you. They were great organisers in their own right. I know it's not just LiUNA but they seem to be particularly good at it, and consistent, and they're very smart people. New recruits, new members, are highly trained, and those with aptitude go up another lever with more training. They are a powerful union, because they use their members, they use their members' power, and they use their own power then in interaction with politicians, with other unions and they represent their members really well. So it was a really interesting learn for me. In recent years they've been over here, passing on their experiences in the mechanics of how to train and hold on to talented people.

I asked Terry would he speak at the 2005 Ard Fheis and at it he made a powerful speech about the links between Ireland and the diaspora and reiterated the support for Sinn Féin's work from the Labour Movement and the Friends of Sinn Féin in the United States. Terry had a wonderful Chief of Staff, Brian Donohue, who's as hard as nails in terms of work and has an Irish sense of humour. Brian also allowed us the use of their space as a venue for receptions, for example around St Patrick's Day, a wonderful place which overlooked the White House. They allowed us it for free.

Before Terry I had met John Samuelsen, a very capable and militant rep and later President of the Transport Workers Union based in New York. His grandmother hailed from Derry, I think. I had met John at a hunger strike exhibition and he had been impressed by the panels which had been designed in Ireland but reproduced in the US. The centenary of the 2013 Dublin Lock-Out, which James Connolly was involved in, was coming up and John asked, 'Could you do an exhibition like you did for the hunger strike?' I said I would do something but it will be much harder, regarding imagery and photographs.

John's office was in a big brownstone building right in the heart of Brooklyn. It was always busy and had a great feel to it of it being a hive of organisation. When you went into John's office, behind his desk was the huge flag of the International Brigade of the Connolly Column, and a little statue of Connolly. There was also an image of a British soldier pointing his weapon at young people on the Falls Road which was from the 1990s. John was a great help to me, especially if I ever needed to pick up people at the airport and get them to their hotels. He'd provide transport, a minibus which had the union logo on the side of the passenger doors. I think John and Terry first met at the St Patrick's Day Parade in New York, yet each were working away separately for the cause of Irish freedom without knowing of each other.

From the time of the hunger strike the Irish American Labor Coalition, inspired by Belfast-born Jim Devine of the Communication Workers of America, had also been active and were very supportive of the campaign calling upon President Clinton to grant Gerry Adams a visa.

I didn't have responsibility for the rest of the US initially, but was later given clearance to travel and visit the major cities so that by the time my visiting status and role had been established Gerry had been granted a designated visa which allowed him to engage in fundraising, with, of course, strict protocols around how the finance was used.

I had also been working with Canadian activists like Alan McConnell for a number of years, even though I couldn't enter Canadian territory because of my outstanding arrest warrant. I would travel up and we would meet close to the border for lunch in Buffalo or upstate Vermont to begin laying the groundwork for what became the highly-successful Friends of Sinn Fein (Canada).

I regularly met Irish-American organisations, small or large, particularly the AOH, many of whose members were also involved with Irish Northern Aid and before that campaigned for civil rights in the North. On the East Coast they were very organised and had a network right through the States. The AOH (Ancient Order of Hibernians) is primarily a Catholic charitable organisation, but they have a 'green' wing which is very active on Ireland.

Some organisations, such as Irish Northern Aid, whilst supportive, wanted to carry on independently, which was their absolute right. With Larry Downes I helped set up 'Unity in Action' and tried to get a rep of each of the Irish-American organisations who were either in New York or near enough to travel to meet once a week while I was there and keep in touch when I wasn't there. Although the Internet had become available, email was only just beginning and it proved a very useful tool in communicating across such a vast territory.

From 1974, Fr Seán McManus's Irish National Caucus played a prominent role in lobbying on Capitol Hill and later with the MacBride Principles' fair employment campaign to combat sectarian discrimination in jobs in the North. In 2010, I brought members of the Ballymurphy Massacre Committee to meet Fr Seán and this later led to the committee's chair, John Teggart, testifying before Congress.

There had been a huge tradition of solidarity campaigns protesting from earlier days, against Bloody Sunday, internment, the criminalisation of prisoners and the hunger strikes of 1980 and 1981, the use of plastic and rubber bullets, Diplock Courts, the strip-searching of women prisoners, the Show Trials, and British collusion with loyalist paramilitaries.

Later, there were campaigns in support of 'on the runs', people like Joe Doherty who had escaped from Crumlin Road Prison in 1981 with seven others. Former escapees who had made their way to the US and quietly settled down, some getting married and having families, lived under fear of detection and being extradited. They were referred to as 'the deportees'. There were many campaigns on their behalf involving great lawyers, many from an Irish background. And central to that work was Nor-Aid. The campaign around Joe Doherty, who was arrested by the FBI in 1983 while he was working in Clancy's Bar in Manhattan, galvanised huge swathes of Irish-American opinion. Over a hundred members of Congress, Cardinal John O'Connor of New York and the city's mayor, David Dinkins, opposed his deportation or extradition. Joe was very well-liked by all those who met him. Celebrities were queuing up to visit him. He spent eight years in the Metropolitan Correctional Center before being sent back to the North where he was imprisoned in the H-Blocks until his release following the signing of the Good Friday Agreement. The street outside the prison in New York where he was held is still named Joe Doherty Way. One of those who worked on his defence (and that of Dessie Macken when he was arrested) was the late Jim Cullen, a former US army general and human rights lawyer, who took over as president of Friends of Sinn Féin in 2012. Jim had also been the first president of the Brehon Law Society, a group which included Irish-American lawyers Paul O'Dwyer and Frank Durkan, who took on Irish republican cases.

Another past president of the Brehons was Marty Glennon who helped establish the Joe Doherty Civil Rights Fellowship along with Sean Crowley (brother of former Congressman Joe Crowley) when they were both law students at CUNY School of Law. To this day the Fellowship sponsors law students' work on civil rights' issues. Marty started out as a union electrician with Local #3 in New York but became a lawyer in order to defend trade unions and their families, and specialises in labour and benefit law. I think it was either Larry Downes or his brother Seán who first introduced us at an Irish Unity conference and we hit it off right away, our politics closely aligning. When I was in New York I'd meet Marty for breakfast or dinner and would often dine at his home with Jenny, his wife, and Caroline and Izzy, their daughters. We would be on the phone so much to each other that the girls referred to me as his 'Irish girlfriend'! His analyses were spot on. I also became friends with Jenny's mother, Linda.

He organised the huge labour delegation which came to Ireland on the centenary of the 1913 Dublin Lockout. He was also helpful in organising a commemoration on the hundredth anniversary of the death of O'Donovan Rossa at Calvary Cemetery in Queens. We had no one to re-enact Pearse's famous graveside oration but Marty suggested his friend, the Belfast actor Tony Devlin for the part. I said, 'Okay, but he better not fuck up!' It was a brilliant choice and I was very pleased with the event. Marty also secured Senator George Mitchell for an event to celebrate the fifteenth anniversary of the Good Friday Agreement.

When I left the US for good, Marty and I still spoke on the phone regularly—just like Larry and I would do—up until I could no longer, given my treatment. I still loved to hear what was happening. He and Jenny visited me last year and he was also here for the quiet celebration of my eightieth birthday.

Years ago, I was thrilled when he told me that he, Jenny, Caroline and Izzy, took part in the big anti-Trump march in New York, but I said to him: 'Tell me you didn't wear those ridiculous looking pink pussyhats!' In 2017 pussyhats were popularised and worn by feminists to protest against the incoming Trump administration and the sexism and chauvinism of Trump. They became an expression of female solidarity and the symbol of collective action—but I still hated them. Later, there was a labour luncheon at Bobby Vans (Joseph Smith's restaurant) sponsored by the James Connolly Irish American Labor Coalition during which Bernadette McCullough, a Teamsters' rep, announced that she would like to make a presentation to Mary Lou and myself—something 'They both love', which is what Marty had told her. Wasn't it the fucking hats and I had to fake my gratitude while Marty sniggered at my discomfort. There is actually still a picture floating around of me wearing one. Have never forgiven Marty!

Mary Lou McDonald modelling those ridiculous-looking pink pussyhats!

John Hume had considerable sway in framing his analysis of the conflict, and how it could be resolved, with politicians such as Edward Kennedy, Daniel Moynihan, Hugh Carey and Tip O'Neill, Speaker of the House of Representatives. While they were critical of the British it is difficult to measure if they curbed British repression—but they got more airtime for their attacks on the republican struggle and did their utmost to deter Irish Americans and others from supporting the republican cause.

In 1979 three priests, Fr Denis Faul, Fr Brian Brady and Fr Raymond Murray, accused the Irish ambassador in Washington, Sean Donlon, of trying to thwart the campaign to free the Birmingham Six by discouraging a congressman, Hamilton Fish Jnr, from taking an interest in this miscarriage of justice. It later emerged that even the Taoiseach at the time, Charles Haughey, suspected Donlon was doing the work of the British Government rather too well in Washington in trying to crush Irish American opposition to what was going on in the North.

Often, the campaigns that have real bite and have the potential for being the most effective, particularly in exposing the Brits and its sectarian state, are the ones which are *most* opposed by those claiming to be champions of justice offering an alternative to physical force.

In the 1980s, Sean MacBride, veteran statesman and Nobel Peace Prize laureate, lent his name to a set of guidelines which called upon US companies to make their investment conditional on fair employment practices, anti-discrimination measures and the promotion of equality. Many senior Irish-American Establishment figures, the Irish Government and its Washington Embassy (led by Sean Donlon), and the SDLP, all opposed and lobbied against the MacBride Principles. One person who deserves a lot of credit for the success of the campaign is Pat Doherty who in the 1980s worked in the office of Harrison Goldin, the New York City comptroller. Doherty's grandfather was a Derry republican who had been imprisoned several times before emigrating to the US in the 1920s.

Despite the resistance to it, the campaign gathered momentum, became a success, left its opponents stranded and looking foolish and spineless. Many cities and states signed up and billions of dollars of public and private investments, conditional on fair employment practices, had a real impact in ensuring nationalists got work, including in places from which they were traditionally excluded. The Principles have now become the congressional standard for all US aid to the North.

Many of the people originally involved in picketing the British Embassy or its consulates-general, ringing into radio shows or in organising tours have since died or long since retired but you find that their daughters and sons and grandchildren are now involved and as enthused about the cause of Irish independence. It's one of the reasons why the republican cause is so powerful and enjoys traction in Washington to this day, particularly support for our position on the Protocol and opposition to British attempts to legislate immunity for themselves and amnesty for their forces over their murderous deeds in the North.

Not surprisingly I kept hearing that the interest a lot of American people had in Ireland had been galvanised by the 1981 hunger strike. For years, they'd been told by the Brits—and Irish Governments—that republicans, the IRA, were all criminals. As if a huge section of the nationalist community woke up one day and went mad. The hunger strike definitely upended that propaganda and was a huge influence, for example, on Richie Neal who is head of the (Congressional) Friends of Ireland Committee.

I remember when I first met Richie he spoke about Bobby Sands. Richie was a young man in Springfield, Massachusetts, in 1981. It had a big Irish and Irish-American community, many who hailed from the Blasket Islands and were Gaeilgeoirí. There were still Irish speakers in Springfield right into the 1980s. But back then he was a councillor in Springfield. He was outraged at Thatcher's treatment of the political prisoners and at the death of Bobby and decided, 'We have to do something here.' He later raised many issues of concern, including the RUC's use of rubber and plastic bullets against civilians, especially children. His influence can also be seen on Nancy Pelosi who as speaker of the House of Representatives said that Congress would block any new trade deal with the UK if Brexit threatened the peace process and the Good Friday Agreement.

He got into hot water in 2022 on a visit to Ireland—over nothing, really. He was criticised by unionists for using the historically-accurate term 'Planter', which unionists used to use regularly with pride.

Most political systems are dominated by people and their like-minded allies who believe that it is their destiny to rule. Richie did not come from such privileged background. His parents died young and he was raised by his grandmother and aunt in fairly poor circumstances, yet through sheer determination he rose to some senior positions in public life.

I became very close to Richie Neal's longtime chief of staff Billy Tranghese, who in a variety of roles had been with Richie since 1989.

Billy helped found the Belfast-Beltway Boxing Project, helping disadvantaged kids in clubs in Belfast with a Washington-based cultural and athletic exchange programme.

My initial function was working on Capitol Hill and briefing both Democrat and Republican representatives and remaining strictly neutral on domestic politics and US foreign policy. In those early visits my immediate task was to find out who was who. I sat about finding out which House members and which Senators, or those among their staff, had an interest in Irish affairs and who would meet you. Very soon I had a good solid list, especially of the Chiefs of Staff. It's such a huge complex that even twenty years later I could still get lost. There are multiple congressional buildings near the Capitol. On one side are some for the House of Representatives and on the other side are some for the Senate. But you get to know or understand eventually. I tried to get to know every House and Senate member's chief of staff personally and would spend time with them in advance of any Sinn Féin visit.

When you're from a small country like ours, it's hard to visualise the sheer size of America, the multiple cultures, the variety of attitudes and stances. It could seem like ten or more very, very different countries. That's the impression I got. You had the South where it was practically tropical. You had Republican Jim Walsh's constituency, Syracuse, where it snowed six months of the year and saw ten feet of snow, and yet at the other end of America it was still balmy.

There's an attitude abroad among many, including some of our own people, that everything about the USA is bad or bullshit. However, I found that by and large people were wonderful, good and kind. Even politicians who had been told we were 'terrorists' would agree to sit and talk and were prepared to have their minds changed once you put the arguments to them.

One of the things that really impressed me about Washington was anybody could walk into the congressional buildings and meet with an aide or leave a letter. You didn't have to make an appointment; you didn't have to say who you were. Of course, physical checks changed after 9/11. The prior openness back then really impressed me. It's a terrible sad thing that the attacks hindered that level of access. It had symbolised the genuine intentions of the people who wrote the original American Constitution who wanted government open to the people. In Leinster House you couldn't get through the door without having somebody vouch for you.

The path to a member of Congress or a Senator was through their aides, advisors, speech writers or Chiefs of Staff. You didn't always have to meet the principal, but if she or he were any good at their job they're going to become interested in an ongoing peace project, its successes or setbacks, because it represents a 'good' cause. The Good Friday Agreement was rightly viewed as an international triumph for President Bill Clinton and the US, its active involvement in the peace process a major success, and especially the role played by Senator George Mitchell in chairing the inter-party talks.

You went up to the Hill and figured out which of the many, identical corridors you were looking for. It meant plenty of walking and plenty of exercise. Given that there were congressional elections every two years you often might have to begin afresh, getting acquainted with new representatives and their staff. I made two friends in two lovely men in charge of admissions—and, remember, they would be dealing with thousands. But they remembered me. They had Irish backgrounds, of course! If they saw Martin and Gerry and I waiting in a long queue, they would send a porter down the line to get us in quicker.

Washington is one of those places where you could go to those god-awful receptions practically every night of the week. I quickly learned to be selective, to go to ones that have any sort of purpose. I went to a lot of those to get known, so that people would know who I was. One of the things I really enjoyed doing was speaking at universities. Many universities in the States have Irish studies groups.

The Brits had spent countless millions in the US trying to present themselves as peace keepers in Ireland and demonising republicans. They were still having a go at us at this time. They were still sending out really nasty attacks on Sinn Féin every day of the week, but often failed to garner interest simply because too many knew enough about Britain's bloody imperialist past. They never mentioned what Loyalism was doing or had ever done and would never admit what British forces had done in the North. Collusion? They pretended that the word was not in the dictionary. I found it a real challenge holding my temper with the Washington embassy even though we were far into the peace process. In those early days they got on as if Thatcher was still prime minister and that nothing had changed in the North.

You know what it told me? It made me so aware of one of the huge difficulties, which has proved to be true, we would always have with the Northern Ireland Office. It made me very aware of what a danger they were to the peace process. It made me more conscious than I had ever been before, having been based in Dublin and not the North and not having to deal directly with the NIO and the many bigots there. The Brits with their disinformation had had a monopoly on the mainstream media, and a huge head start. The only people I remember that had somebody in the North on the ground reporting for them was one of the Boston papers. I think it was the *Boston Herald*. The *Boston Globe* also did at one point, with Kevin Cullen. The other views Americans received were from stringers based in London or who worked for the British press. The whole thing was totally skewed. Some of it was actually misinformation and the awful thing was that some of it was not even intentionally so because they were doing it through this totally British perspective. They did not even get what was going on.

I visited many of the main newspapers and spoke to senior journalists. In addition, I met with many of the regional papers because regional papers are more read around the US than the *Wall Street Journal*, for example. I think the Brits ultimately just gave up and, besides, they had a valuable proxy in the Irish Government which often threw their snowballs for them.

Individual Irish officials we got on with, sometimes those who had direct experience of the North through the old Maryfield Secretariat or the Foreign Affairs department, which could not but have opened some of their eyes to what life was like for nationalists under British rule. But many officials viewed Sinn Féin as the enemy (rather than the British, controlling part of Ireland) and they were obsessed with counteracting both our progress and the growing pro-unity sentiment.

In 2013, Ciarán Staunton was interviewed on RTÉ by Myles Dungan. Ciarán, originally from Mayo, had helped organise the Irish Immigration Reform Movement in the US in the late 1980s which helped secure the Morrison Bill. It was named after Senator Bruce Morrison and it granted legal status to over 200,000 undocumented Irish. Ciarán later discovered that the Department of Foreign Affairs Consul General in New York had instructed his staff to have the RTÉ interview transcribed. It was sent to a staffer in Kuala Lumpur, Malaysia, who sent back the full (nine-page) interview. The Anglo-Irish head keeping tabs on an Irish-American community leader is one example of the type of time-wasting monitoring officials are involved in.

For over two decades both Fianna Fáil and Fine Gael had a fundraising arm in the US, accepting donations big and small from rich donors and sympathisers. During this period Fianna Fáil collected over one million dollars. Before Bertie Ahern donned his tuxedo as the guest speaker on the dinner circuit, Charlie Haughey had been the star attraction. Both parties had no issue with fund-raising for their organisations back home in Ireland. No issue, that is, until Friends of Sinn Féin (USA) came on the scene and honed its fund-raising capabilities.

The story is so familiar.

Every time that Irish republicans advance, within the establishment's rulebook, the powers-that-be change the rules. Thatcher amended the law to ban prisoners from standing for election because Bobby Sands was elected MP for Fermanagh and South Tyrone. The British introduced an oath for council candidates (having to forswear 'the use of violence'), increased the deposit to stand in election, introduced compulsory ID, all aimed at futilely inhibiting the growth of Sinn Féin.

So successful was Friends of Sinn Féin that Bertie Ahern, as Taoiseach in 2001, amended the Irish Electoral Act prohibiting political parties from accepting foreign donations. It was a blatant reaction to Sinn Féin being more popular and being taken more seriously than Fianna Fáil by the Irish diaspora and other supporters. In twenty years, sympathisers in the USA donated ten times the amount to Sinn Féin than Fianna Fáil had raised over thirty years.

However, some in Fine Gael, not satisfied with the ban on foreign donations, have called for legislation which would see the state contribution to political parties (based on their electoral strength) withdrawn from Sinn Féin.

I was back home towards the end of summer 2001. The family and I, along with Larry Downes, were all on Achill Island thoroughly enjoying ourselves when news came through about the arrest of three Irish men in Bogota—who came to be known as the Colombia Three. I was immediately called back to Dublin, Brendan dropping Larry and I off at the train station in Westport. As further news came through, Larry was devastated and we were both concerned, seriously worried, that all the moral and political support we had been garnering towards Irish unity would be undermined, would be scuttled (regardless of what explanation was proffered for the three Republicans being in Colombia). And that's what happened when I returned to the US. Doors were closed, congressional aides were no longer available and it was to take many, many years of painstaking persuasion and proofs that the Movement was wedded to the peace process, to bring that support back. We lost one big donor permanently, and he said, 'I just don't trust you.' I was asked a hundred times, 'What's going on?' and was told numerous times that you can't ride two horses at once. It would have been academic—and I'm not—to attempt an explanation or defence. To be fair, later, many of those who had felt let down did renew contact, reopened the doors and became one again vocal and active in their support for Irish unity and the republican project.

We usually got into the office by eight or half eight in the morning. On this particular Tuesday morning we got in sometime before nine. The phone was ringing: it was Greg's mother, Paula, calling from New York to see if he was safe. She said a plane had flown into the World Trade Centre. Our first reaction was to laugh it off and I chimed in that Paula was overreacting. I used to describe her as 'the mammiest-mam' and we both thought she was being melodramatic. But she called back a few minutes later and said that a second plane had hit the towers—and they weren't small planes. She said the news was describing it as a possible attack and that Greg needed to get somewhere safe. We didn't have a TV in the office but Greg's apartment was just a few blocks away so we decided to walk to it.

Our office was four blocks from Senate Office Buildings. At this hour, Stanton Park was usually empty as people were now at work. But we noticed how many people were walking through the park, dozens and dozens of people hurriedly moving along. Staffers were walking very quickly away from the capitol and there was a sense of panic. We got to Greg's apartment and turned on the TV to watch the news and were both astonished and shocked at what was happening. Then there was news of the Pentagon being hit by another plane. We went outside to look around and saw more staffers and people rushing to get out of the city which was in a state of emergency and being evacuated. We could see smoke from the direction of the Pentagon which was only a couple of miles away, as the crow flies.

Greg's wife Meghan, the office manager for the Irish American Unity Conference, had gone to work at her office at the National Press Club. Telecommunications were down. I couldn't phone Brendan, whom I later learnt, was frantically trying to get through to me as he'd seen the attacks on the news. Greg repeatedly tried to call Meghan. She had left work and cycled through all the traffic, the bedlam, and the many accidents to eventually join us. Sirens were constantly wailing. It was just a nightmare.

I was supposed to go back to my cousin Pat's house but all the trains had stopped, so I waited. A few hours later we walked around Capitol Hill. An eerie calm had replaced the earlier overwhelming panic. The sun was shining: it was gorgeous—such an anomaly. No one among the people we saw had a clue what was going on but there were exchanges about whether loved ones were caught up in the Pentagon explosion or in the World Trade Centre.

Greg, a political activist in his own right, as well as working for the Irish cause, had been proudly involved just a few months earlier with the Mobilization for Global Justice (MGJ) organisation which had staged the major anti-globalisation protests across the States and successfully disrupted the spring meeting of the IMF and the World Bank.

Instinctively, I knew that the MGT's progress was probably finished—would be deemed as anti-American—and that the US would swing to the right as a result of the attacks, regardless of who was behind them, and that many causes, including our own, would suffer or be less tolerated. Greg, at first, didn't believe me, but that is what happened.

Washington adopted a war-footing and stayed that way for a long time. Armoured cars and vehicles appeared on many street corners and batteries of surface-to-air missiles were parked adjacent to important buildings. Bollards and gates were erected everywhere.

CHAPTER TWELVE

JAMES CONNOLLY

Of all my American work the project of which I am proudest, and which I would have loved Billy, my Da, to have seen, was the successful Transatlantic campaign to build and locate a James Connolly Museum (Áras Uí Chonghaile: James Connolly Visitor Centre), just three blocks away on the Falls from where Connolly and his family lived. As a teenager on my way to school I would pass a house on Glenalina Terrace on the Falls Road, opposite the front gates of the City Cemetery. It was locally a famous landmark because it was here that James Connolly lived when he returned to Ireland from the USA in December 1910. In 1968 on the centenary of Connolly's birth a bust of Connolly was unveiled above the entrance by his son Roddy. Connolly and his eldest daughter Nora had moved into this three-storey house before being joined by his wife Lily and the rest of the children. I got to know Nora well when I moved to Dublin in 1972. Her account of her last meeting with her father a few hours before he was executed is heart-breaking. Nora, who was very active in republican circles in Belfast, had brought Pearse to the city to speak at St Mary's Hall. The Connolly family were still living at Glenalina Terrace at the time of Connolly's execution in 1916.

In Belfast, Connolly had joined the Irish Transport Workers' Union and was advocating an Irish Labour Party whereas others were advocating support for the British Labour Party on the basis that raising the 'Irish Question' would only 'divide' workers. He saw through that and was of the opinion that linking to a British party was 'a subjugation' which would only prolong the connection with England. He was a powerful advocate for the working class and won increases in pay and shorter working hours for striking dockers. He helped organise striking mill girls fight for better conditions: at work they were fined for laughing or singing or fixing their hair. He welcomed the prospect of

Home Rule, even with its huge shortcomings. He got a great insight into the reactionary forces in Belfast. His strikes were demonised as 'Fenian' and 'Papist' plots—the usual. The RIC prevented him from canvassing in Protestant working-class areas when he unsuccessfully stood for election in the Docks ward.

Writing in the *Irish Worker* in May 1914 he warned that partition and the 'betrayal of the national democracy of industrial Ulster would mean a carnival of reaction both North and South, would set back the wheels of progress, would destroy the oncoming unity of the Irish Labour movement and paralyse all advanced movements whilst it endured.'

Prophetic and hugely prescient.

I had been liaising with trade unions in the USA for many years and had been surprised to discover that there were no official or even unofficial contacts between trade unionists in Ireland and the United States. It surprised me because of the deep Irish connections that go back to the founding of some of America's most militant and radical trade unions, including Connolly himself who spent a number of years organising on the east coast of the US.

Take Mike Quill, for example, an anti-Treaty IRA activist from County Kerry, who like many others was forced into exile following the Civil War and found his way to New York. Here he got work, like so many other Irish emigrants, in New York City's transport system. Very quickly, along with a number of former IRA comrades, he became involved in unionising workers in the subway system. Although physically attacked and vilified they stood firm and founded the Transport Workers Union in 1934, specifically naming and modelling it after the Irish Transport and General Workers Union. The TWU now represents over 150,000 members across airline, railroad, transit and other areas. My good friend John Samuelsen, President of the Transport Workers Union, has pointed out that it was no accident that so many founding TWU members were former IRA men. He said these men were often battle-hardened and weren't afraid to take on the Pinkertons (a private detective agency), whose union-busting tactics were very often violent.

Such was the status of Mike Quill when he died in 1966 that Martin Luther King remarked: 'Mike Quill was a fighter for decent things all his life—Irish independence, labour organisation and racial equality. He has spent his life ripping the chains of bondage off his fellow man. This is a man the ages will remember.'

Gerry asked me to work with Harry Connolly to help secure financial support to open a James Connolly Visitor Centre in West Belfast. I was delighted to be able to introduce him to two fantastic supporters of Irish unity, John Samuelsen, and Terry O'Sullivan, President of LiUNA. Harry is the Director of Fáilte Feirste Thiar (Welcome to West Belfast), an organisation established post-ceasefire to encourage tourists to discover and visit the west of the city, and ensure that the social and economic benefits of tourism would be felt in local neighbourhoods and local communities.

He and former prisoner and trade unionist, Jim McVeigh, were both working on a project to build a Connolly Visitor Centre and already had support from Belfast City Council. But that wasn't enough to get the project off the ground.

The idea of the centre began gathering a head of steam on the centenary of the 1916 Rising when delegates from various unions visited Dublin. They then went up to Belfast to participate in the Easter Parade to the Republican Plot in Milltown Cemetery. Their trip also coincided with the unveiling of a statue of James Connolly outside the office of the Falls Community Council on Good Friday. Terry was invited to speak at the gathering of about 1,500 people. I know him to be a powerful orator, some would say a fiery orator. At the unveiling he referred to his favourite Connolly quote: 'The cause of Labour is the cause of Ireland. The cause of Ireland is the cause of Labour. They cannot be dissevered.'

Harry spoke to Terry about their dream of opening an interpretative visitor centre and museum dedicated to Connolly. So they immediately walked up the Falls Road to a derelict and rundown building, not far from where Connolly had lived. Terry asked if they owned the building and Harry said they did not.

'Buy the building and you'll have skin in the game and we'll help you raise the rest,' Terry said.

From the City Hall—Jim McVeigh led the quite powerful Sinn Féin group on the council—they secured £250,000 to buy the building. That alone is extraordinary when you consider how our first councillors were demeaned, demonised and illegally excluded from council business just twenty years earlier, as well as being subject to attempts on their lives, including their city hall offices being bombed.

Afterwards, Harry came to me, excited about the prospects. So I stared him in the eye and said, 'If you want to do this, don't fuck it up!'

And he didn't. And our American comrades delivered.

President Michael D Higgins opening Áras Uí Chonghaile, 2019

In 2017 I had set up a meeting in LiUNA headquarters in Washington attended by Harry, Kevin Gamble (director of Féile an Phobail), and the MP for West Belfast Paul Maskey. I was thorough with them on how to approach the unions and their organisers. Never cold call. Always email or text in advance. Show good manners. And when putting proposals in writing or making presentations make sure you use good grammar—a bugbear of mine from school and my *An Phoblacht* days which, I'm glad to say, Mary Lou shares! I checked everything!

A delegation, including some family members, came over from the States for eight days in 2019 and were hosted by the Movement. They visited Crumlin Road Jail and went to a variety of talks and met with people like the late Bobby Storey. A multi-award-winning firm, McGurk Architects from South Derry, was brought in to design the centre. I think the grandfather of the project manager, Colm McGurk, was among those rounded up in 1916 and interned in Frongoch in Wales. I was kept in the loop throughout.

Conway Mill in the Falls, where Connolly had organised the mill girls, was the starting point for a big march on Good Friday in April 2019, involving trade union representatives, including the US delegation, and several hundred local republicans. They proceeded to the new centre, Áras Ui Chonghaile, for the official opening by President Michael D Higgins at which Terry O'Sullivan and John

Samuelsen raised the flag of the Irish Citizen Army. In the end I believe up to nineteen sponsoring trade unions from across North America contributed to its construction. If we hadn't forged those links with the trade union movement in the US, it would never have happened. I couldn't be there for the opening because of my ban but on Easter Saturday night Sinn Féin Mayor Deirdre Hargey hosted a civic dinner in the City Hall for the American delegation and at that my granddaughter Aoife accepted on my behalf a small statuette of James Connolly, based on the larger statue that stands outside Áras.

As I said, I just wish that Billy, my Da, had been alive to see it opening. I think he would have been very proud.

My health was deteriorating; my cancer had returned. Some years after I was shot I had to have more surgery for abdominal injuries. My body had suffered a great degree of trauma. My first cancer diagnosis was in 1996. Now, it has moved from my lung to my liver to my bone, all from the original breast cancer, I'm sure.

After almost twenty-one years my 'two years' stint in the US was coming to an end and a replacement had to be found. One person stood out—Ciaran Quinn from Belfast, now living in Dublin with his wife, a doctor, and their two children.

Ciaran had grown up in Riverdale not far from where I had lived in Ladybrook.

In the same month that I was shot in 1971 two brothers, John Quinn (Ciaran's father) and Jimmy (his uncle), were arrested in possession of arms. In Andersonstown and Springfield Road Barracks they were horrifically tortured for several days. They had been stripped, blindfolded and subjected to mock executions and drowning. They also suffered multiple stab wounds, bruises and lacerations and had cigarettes stubbed out on their bodies. Attempts were made to administer electric shocks to John Quinn and insert a rifle into his anus. He was dumped naked in a freezing coal bunker where he was left for hours. The two brothers were convicted and served their sentences as political prisoners in the cages of Long Kesh. Ciaran was just a child at the time.

The first time I met Ciaran was in 1999 at the Ard Fheis which was being held in the RDS. This tall fella approached me and asked me did I know where he could find Gerry. I replied: 'Why? Who de fuck are you?' He explained that he worked for Gerry and we both started laughing. He asked me if I always spoke to strangers that way and I said, 'Only republicans.' We subsequently worked well together on the ard comhairle as Ciaran had various roles, including leas Ard Rúnaí and Director of Publicity.

Ciaran had also been Chief of Staff in Martin's deputy First Minister's Office. Together we had coordinated Martin's trips to the US which included three meetings in the White House with Obama. On another occasion Martin—who was extremely busy at Stormont—was to be the keynote speaker at the Friends of Sinn Féin Dinner in New York. Ciaran and Martin came straight to the venue from the airport and Martin spoke as starters were being served. I then had to tap Ciaran on the shoulder to tell them their lift to the airport was outside. They were five hours in New York and never even got their dinner.

During the transition to Mary Lou taking over from Gerry as president Ciaran acted as her temporary Chief of Staff and together we organised her visits to Capitol Hill, the State Department, the National Security Council and to Friends of Sinn Féin receptions. We also worked together countering the biggest threat to the Good Friday Agreement, the decision by Britain to leave the European Union. Brexit would be taking the North out of the EU despite the majority vote in the North to remain. The DUP calculated that it presented an opportunity to undermine the Good Friday Agreement, which it had never supported, by accentuating social, economic and political differences between North and South which might also lead to the reintroduction of a hard border.

In August or September 2019 I met Ciaran in a coffee shop on Dawson Street. As I was explaining the responsibilities and challenges of the job I thought he looked overawed and was panicking. I told him that I was glad it was him as I trusted him.

Then I added, 'Just don't fuck it up.'

He hasn't.

I began by introducing him to the US embassy staff, then to Congressional people, reps and their aides, and our supporters. We travelled around the US for five weeks. I also told him who to avoid! The key was to be honest, never try to sell them a lie, and always treat them with respect, because these are people who go over and above to support us. On another occasion, when Mary Lou was to speak at a Friends of Sinn Féin dinner, we went through Ciaran's speech in her hotel room over a bottle of wine and took out all the grammatical errors—which he took well, I think. What I didn't know was that Ciaran and Mary Lou had introduced a very flattering section on me which they kept secret. That would never have got past me.

Covid kicked in a few months later and resulted in an end to all travelling but before that there was a reception held in my honour in Washington which was attended by Richie Neal and Eliot Engel, Chair of the Foreign Relations Committee.

Ciaran took over in January 2020.

I am very, very proud of my work on behalf of our cause in the US, the many, many friends I made, their hospitality, their generosity, the time they gave to defend peace and promote freedom, their continued unswerving support. There wouldn't be space to mention them all and to this day they will phone me to ask how I am keeping, how I am coping. Those friendships are powerful and comforting.

Above all, my dear, dear friend Larry Downes calls me every day from New York without fail.

CHAPTER THIRTEEN

THE END

My mother Maureen and Billy would come visit us in Dublin and also go on holidays with us. They loved Achill because it was a place where they had honeymooned. As Maureen's health deteriorated I saw less of her. She died in December 1996—and her sister Kathleen, my cousin Pat's mother, died just six weeks later. I couldn't go to the wake in Norfolk Drive, nor to my mother's funeral, but before her burial Dessie Macken and the Movement arranged with a Belfast undertaker for her remains to be brought to Dundalk. At Dixon's Funeral Home in a Chapel of Rest the coffin was opened and we held a little ceremony at which I said a few words and paid tribute to her and to Billy, who had also travelled with the cortege. Terry and Frances were with me, as was Brendan and my brother Alan and Mary. I think I said something like, 'I got my politics from my father, but I got my courage from my mother.' I then had about half an hour alone with her before the funeral party crossed the border for mass in St Nicholas Church and burial in the adjacent cemetery beside the graves of her family in Ardglass.

A week later a former RUC Special Branch officer was speaking at a DUP meeting. He said there were reports that Rita O'Hare had been in the North for her mother's funeral and that if he had known he would personally have arrested her. They never gave up; vengeful to the very end.

My brother Bill died in England in May 1998 when I was in the USA. Brendan phoned to my hotel and Gerry answered the phone first. Then I heard the news. I cut short my stay and came home but, as is the practice in England, where bodies can remain in a freezer for weeks, the funeral was not immediate and Billy had an agonising wait. This greatly upset Billy and me. I couldn't of course go to Bill's funeral either, to condole with his wife Linda and daughters Jessie and Rachel.

Billy was now on his own, though fiercely independent, and we thought perhaps he could come and live with us. For a while he was actually still driving, which I wasn't happy about, and he came down every few weeks and stayed for a few days. He had always been a handyman and liked to be active with a screwdriver or a hammer, the electrics or anything mechanical, and Brendan watched him like a hawk! To this day when you turn the light on in my little office in the front room you can still get an electric shock. We call it the 'fuck-you, Billy' switch.

He had many visitors in Norfolk. Terry's son Kevin sometimes stayed. Gerry and Colette Adams lived next door. And on Sundays, using at first a stick and then a frame he'd walk down the street to dinner in Danny and Leslie's or the three of them went for a drive to County Down or across to Carlingford. Alan's wife Mary and their kids called in regularly. After he could no longer use the car many of our friends provided an army of chauffeurs. He protested at all this attention but I knew he was secretly delighted and grateful, despite it being a sign of his diminishing freedom. These volunteers included Dawn Doyle and Mark McLernon. Billy absolutely adored Mark; thought he was hilarious. Lucilita Bhreatnach and Mick O'Brien also brought him up and down. He'd stay for a few days or for a weekend but did not want to live here. Dawn told me that on one occasion when she went to Norfolk to get him there was no answer. She went around the side of the house and saw a ladder precariously propped up against the back wall. Billy was on the roof fixing a tile and was attached to the ladder by a bungee cord. He was ninety years of age!

He was also a prolific correspondent and would sit at his table in his living room well after midnight writing to friends, old and new.

We had planned an extended stay with us but it didn't work out. He wasn't used to the hustle and bustle and the noise of kids throughout the house and was tetchy and unsettled. He also thought he would have more time with me to sit, reminisce, and discuss poetry, which he loved. But I had to divide my time between Brendan and the family and work as well. On one occasion all the family were on holiday in Achill and Brendan and I decided to have some time on our own. So, we went for a walk which included the famine-era Deserted Village and taking in Slievemore. On the mountain we looked back and saw another hill walker, quite a distance away but going at a fair pace. Brendan joked, 'It's probably, fucking Billy.' And it was! But to be fair to Billy he was actually delivering a message and said I was to ring Gerry Adams at a number written on the bit of paper he was clutching. There was some crisis or another. I can't remember clearly if this was over the Colombia

Three (when I'm certain Larry was on Achill with us)—or some one of the many other crises that bedevil peace processes.

We discussed building an annexe where Billy could have his own place and could come in and out as he pleased but Brendan worked out that the cost was beyond our means unless Billy sold Norfolk Drive. He did not want to do that so he went home to Belfast.

There obviously comes a point in all our lives when you are no longer able to live independently. Billy, who was now ninety-one, was becoming forgetful and food left for him in the fridge would gather blue mould. It was a huge blow to his morale that he was no longer active. Alan and Mary, myself, and our Terry, who lived in Belfast, and Billy's friends, were becoming quite concerned. He spent two weeks in Nazareth House, off the Ravenhill Road, and then moved to Glenowen Court Care Home in Andersonstown for respite. But even there he had falls in the privacy of his room and ended up in the City Hospital twice. It was a constant worry and a decision had to be made about where was best for him and finally he moved into Slieve Dhu Nursing Home in Newcastle, just below Slieve Donard and the Mournes, places which he had loved and which reminded him of our childhood holidays. There was a bright lounge where he could sit and read and he could discuss books with another resident, Winnie Neeson, a former teacher from Banbridge who had lived in the Falls in the Forties during the war. The staff were very kind and nice to him and it was close enough to Belfast for people to visit. Alan and Mary lived just a few miles away.

His condition rapidly declined over the following two months. He ate little, was now confined to bed, and slept most of the day. It was nearing the end and I wanted to see him and was concerned that I wouldn't get there on time. This was May 2003. I told Padraic Wilson about my plans. We both knew that if I was arrested on a historical charge going back thirty years and was imprisoned it would be a bit of a political fuck-up. Unionists would rejoice and republicans would be infuriated. But I didn't really care if I was arrested, though I would take precautions.

It was Siobhán O'Hanlon who organised everything. She and Pat picked up Brendan and me in their car. We drove north and just before the border, in a layby outside Omeath, she gave me one of her wigs to wear, to disguise my distinctive red hair. Siobhan herself had been undergoing chemo and wore a wig after she lost her beautiful long hair. From the border it wasn't far; about twenty miles. I loved the scenery, the old walls, the forests, the sheep grazing peacefully. From Newry we drove through Mayobridge and Hilltown, crossing the Mournes and down into the seaside town of Newcastle.

Siobhán and Pat waited outside Slieve Dhu and Brendan and I went in. Billy was in a bed and was far gone. He'd only a short time to live. I took off my wig and said, 'It's me, Rita,' and then he opened his eyes and recognised me and we hugged. Then, in typical Billy fashion, he said, 'I think I'm fucked.' Brendan left us alone and I just sat with Billy and thought about everything. Everything. Our lives and how close we always were. Walking with him in the Falls Park. The long hikes— Billy's famous 'death marches'—across the mountains behind us when we were all together as a family. Being separated from him and Maureen, not able to go home—all of it. I had been determined to make this visit regardless of what could happen. No one was going to stop me from seeing Billy, my oul Da, for the last time, and saying goodbye.

Rita with Billy at Tullaree, below Slieve Donard, c.1953

ACKNOWLEDGMENTS

Greenisland Press would like to acknowledge the following people for their contributions to Rita's memoir: Brendan Brownlee, Mick Nolan, Síle Darragh, Mark Dawson, Patricia Freedman, Larry Downes, Greg O'Loughlin, John Donnelly, Gerry Adams, Harry Connolly.

INDEX

Greenisland Press is an Irish imprint of Elsinor Verlag (Coesfeld, Germany) and is a not-for-profit publishing house. Other books available from Greenisland Press:

POLITICS/HISTORY

Free Statism and The Good Old IRA – Danny Morrison

Rewriting The Troubles – Dr Patrick Anderson

Curious Journey – The IRA and Cumann na mBan, 1916-1923 – Timothy O'Grady

Captive Columns: An Underground Prison Press, 1865—2000 – Eoghan Mac Cormaic

POETRY

the pen behind the wire, prison poems 1982-91 – Eoghan Mac Cormaic

NOVELS

McCoubrey – Mark B. McCaffery

Longlines – Caoilte Breatnach